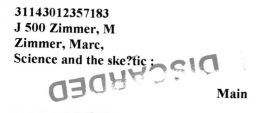

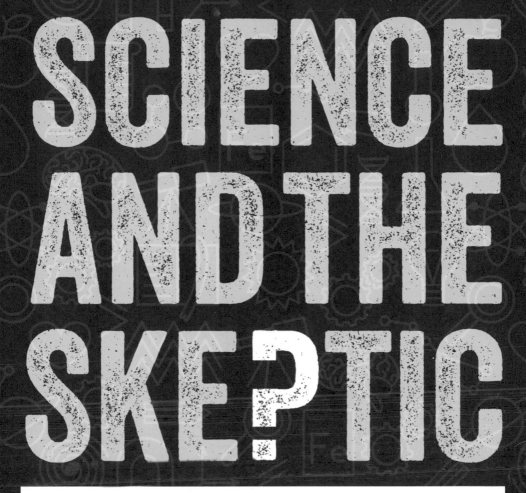

SCIENCE AND THE SKEPTIC

DISCERNING FACT FROM FICTION

MARC ZIMMER

Twenty-First Century Books / Minneapolis

To my father

Twenty-First Century Books™
An imprint of Lerner Publishing Group, Inc.
241 First Avenue North
Minneapolis, MN 55401 USA

For reading levels and more information, look up this title at www.lernerbooks.com.

Main body text set in Avenir LT Pro.
Typeface provided by Linotype AG.

Library of Congress Cataloging-in-Publication Data

Names: Zimmer, Marc, author.
Title: Science and the skeptic : discerning fact from fiction / Marc Zimmer.
Description: Minneapolis : Twenty-First Century Books, [2022] | Includes
    bibliographical references and index. | Audience: Ages 13–18 | Audience:
    Grades 10–12 | Summary: "Covering how science is done, why some people
    want to trick others, and why false information can be dangerous, this book
    empowers readers to know which sources to trust and which to dismiss as
    deceit"— Provided by publisher.
Identifiers: LCCN 2021013452 (print) | LCCN 2021013453 (ebook) |
    ISBN 9781728419459 (library binding) | ISBN 9781728445434 (ebook)
Subjects: LCSH: Science—Juvenile literature. | Pseudoscience—Juvenile
    literature. | Fraud in science—Juvenile literature.
Classification: LCC Q163 .Z55 2022 (print) | LCC Q163 (ebook) | DDC 500—
    dc23

LC record available at https://lccn.loc.gov/2021013452
LC ebook record available at https://lccn.loc.gov/2021013453

Manufactured in the United States of America
1-49068-49266-8/30/2021

CONTENTS

CHAPTER 1

WHAT IS SCIENCE?

To distinguish between science and fake science, we need to know what science is. Science has many definitions, but most people agree that science is the process of understanding the natural world by interpreting the results of experiments.

Before 1833 people who conducted experiments—those who mixed, observed, and synthesized chemicals—were called natural philosophers. Famous figures such as Galen (ca. 129–210), Galileo Galilei (1564–1642), and Sir Isaac Newton (1642–1727) were all natural philosophers. The term *science* existed, but there was no common term for all the people who did science. In 1833 William Whewell, a professor at Cambridge University, coined the term *scientist* to highlight that these were empirical folks, people who relied on experiments to build knowledge, rather than philosophers, or people who dealt strictly with ideas.

Generally, scientists follow the scientific method to discover facts about nature. In this procedure, scientists begin with all the knowledge they already have to make an educated guess, or a hypothesis, about a new observation or phenomenon that has yet to be explained. According to the philosopher of science Karl Popper (1902–1994), for a hypothesis to be truly scientific, there must be an experiment that would disprove it. For example, scientists cannot conduct an experiment that would show whether a sunset is beautiful or not, because there is no way to prove or disprove beauty. Therefore, the study of beauty is not science.

But the study of gravitational waves, ripples in space-time that are produced by massive objects moving at extreme accelerations, such as colliding black holes, is science. When Albert Einstein (1879–1955) hypothesized the existence of gravitational waves in 1916, he didn't think we would ever be able to detect these waves because they are so minute. In theory (and in practice), gravitational waves regularly pass through us and stretch and squeeze us by amounts so small that we can't feel the changes. Despite this hurdle, their existence was provable—all scientists had to do was create the technology needed to measure such tiny changes. In 2015, as a result of the world's largest and most expensive experiment, scientists measured gravitational waves for the first time. The waves had traveled for 1.3 billion years before passing Earth on their way through space. It took billions of dollars and almost one thousand people to prove that gravitational waves from faraway, massive objects in space hit Earth every few weeks. Since then, scientists have detected them regularly. Because the existence of these strange, barely detectable waves was disprovable, the prediction that they existed was a scientific hypothesis. Once scientists measured and detected them, their existence became scientific fact. If the experiment had not detected gravitational waves, then the existence of the waves would have been disproven and the hypothesis would have been wrong.

After conducting an experiment, scientists interpret the results and decide if they proved the hypothesis. Usually, experimental results come in the form of measurements. To detect gravitational waves, scientists from the United States, the United Kingdom, Germany, and Australia collaborated on the Laser Interferometer Gravitational-Wave Observatory (LIGO). LIGO consists of two 2.5-mile-long (4 km) L-shaped vacuum chambers. One is in Louisiana, and the other is 1,865 miles (3,002 km) away in Washington State. The vacuum chambers are housed in 12-foot-tall (3.6 m) concrete pipes that have to be raised a little less than 3 feet (1 m) at their ends to account for Earth's curvature. Gravitational waves that originate billions of light-years from Earth distort the 2.5-mile-long mirror spacing at the ends of the vacuum chambers by about 0.001 times the width of a proton. To ensure these minuscule distortions aren't caused by local car crashes, earthquakes, and other disturbances on Earth, the two LIGO detectors were constructed far apart. Therefore, if the scientists observed the same distortion at both LIGO detectors and the distortions occurred ten milliseconds apart (the time it takes to travel 1,865 miles [3,002 km] at the speed of light), then they had detected a gravitational wave.

On Monday, September 14, 2015, at 4:51 a.m. in Louisiana, a gravitational wave arrived from 1.3 billion light-years away, stretching and squeezing space itself, including the lasers, first

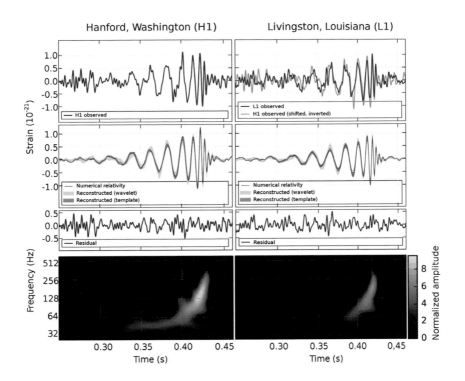

Hanford, Washington (H1)   Livingston, Louisiana (L1)

Pictured above are the results from the September 2015 LIGO detection of gravitational waves. Both detectors saw an increase in the intensity of the wave signal, corresponding to the merging of two black holes. The signals were observed about seven milliseconds apart, the time it took for the waves to travel the 1,865 miles (3,002 km) between the two LIGO sites.

at the Louisiana site and then seven milliseconds later at the Washington site. Everyone involved with the project in the United States was sleeping. In Germany it was 11:51 a.m., time for lunch. Marco Drago, a young physicist working at the Max Planck Institute for Gravitational Physics in Hannover, Germany, looked at the data coming from LIGO. He immediately recognized the gravitational wave pattern predicted by computer simulations. One of Drago's colleagues contacted the LIGO operations room in Louisiana. Everyone was sworn to secrecy while the LIGO researchers checked and rechecked the data. The signal wasn't a test, and it wasn't noise. It was the real thing, a gravitational wave. By February 2016, five months after the signal was observed, everyone involved was convinced it was real, and the researchers held a press conference to announce that they had detected Einstein's gravitational waves. Meanwhile, they published a paper in *Physical Review Letters* describing the findings. It had more than one thousand authors.

Technologies and instruments used to take measurements, such as LIGO, are never perfect and will always introduce experimental uncertainties. Uncertainties are an inherent component of scientific experimentation. In detecting gravitational waves, the uncertainties were because gravitational waves cause such a small change, a change that barely stood out against the background noise. That and checking to make sure the detection wasn't a prank or a mistake is why the researchers took five months to convince themselves that what they had measured was real. When they reported their results, they made sure to include the uncertainties. Since then, more gravitational observatories have been constructed and many more gravitational waves have been detected. Critics of science sometimes disparage scientific results because of the included uncertainties, often shown as "error bars." They argue that the uncertainties mean that scientists don't know anything for sure. This is a mistake born from a lack of understanding. Without errors and uncertainty, there would be no science.

SCIENTIFIC FEATS

Science has made incredible discoveries, some of them even lifesaving. The finding that has saved the most lives is

Abel Wolman and Linn Enslow's 1918 discovery that water can be disinfected by chlorination. This discovery, and its implementation in producing safe, clean water, has saved almost two hundred million lives. Next is William Foege's smallpox eradication strategy, developed in the 1970s. It has also saved hundreds of millions of lives. Third would be Maurice Hilleman's development of forty vaccines during the mid-twentieth century. Among them are eight that are commonly used today (including measles, mumps, and chicken pox vaccines). These eight vaccines are estimated to save eight million lives each year.

Keeping track of the number of lives saved is one great way of quantifying the importance of a scientific discovery. Another way is to analyze whether the discovery was a scientific breakthrough, a finding that revolutionized entire scientific fields or led scientists to even more incredible discoveries. While water chlorination, smallpox eradication, and vaccines have certainly changed our lives for the better, they have not changed the way science is done or improved our understanding of science itself. This is why none of these four scientists have been awarded a Nobel Prize.

Nobel Prizes are the most prestigious awards in the world. Nobel Prizes in Chemistry, Physics, and Medicine are awarded for the most remarkable scientific breakthroughs. Nobel laureates, the people who win Nobel Prizes, earn a hefty sum of money in addition to a diploma, a gold medal, and global prestige. You can identify top scientific breakthroughs by looking at the Nobel laureates. Most major scientific breakthroughs have been rewarded with Nobel Prizes.

However, Nobel Prizes are not always awarded objectively. Women and Black scientists are not proportionally represented among the laureates. James Watson, Francis Crick, and Maurice

Wilkins (who helped discover the double helical structure of DNA) and Einstein (for his discovery of the photoelectric effect) deservedly received Nobel Prizes. However, in the past, the Nobel Foundation unfairly ignored scientists such as Lise Meitner, one of the four scientists to discover nuclear fission. Her adviser, Otto Hahn, got the Nobel Chemistry award in 1944 for her work. Recently the Nobel Foundation has made an effort to acknowledge the work of outstanding women scientists.

There is no correct way of ranking scientific discoveries, but no matter how you rank them, they have all relied on the groundwork of others. It is incredibly rare that discoveries occur in a vacuum. As Newton famously said, "[We stand] on the shoulders of giants." Scientists have to trust the science they build on, and so truth and facts are central to the workings of science.

The amount of scientific misinformation (errors introduced by accident) and disinformation (falsehoods propagated on purpose) is rapidly increasing. Scientific progress comes under threat when scientists don't know whether the science they rely on is true. Then scientists often have to spend more time and effort verifying information that purports to be science, instead of testing new hypotheses.

It is not just scientists that have to fact-check science. Everybody needs to be able to distinguish real science from fake science—not just to do science but also to live safe and productive lives. We need to know whether the supplements advertised on TV work or whether they are a waste of money. Whether vaccines will protect us from diseases or whether climate change is worth trying to fix. And sometimes we just want to know whether researchers really are doing something as unbelievable as genetically engineering Asian elephants to re-create woolly mammoths. (As with Harvard's Woolly

Mammoth Revival project, which is trying to bring back woolly mammoths in an attempt to restore ancient ecosystems.)

THE JIGSAW PUZZLE OF SCIENCE

Nature is full of intriguing puzzles for scientists to solve, but the pieces to the puzzles don't come in a box with the number of pieces listed and a picture of the solution on the lid. To solve any of nature's puzzles, scientists need to find the pieces and put them in the correct place. Some puzzles are much more important than others, and within the puzzles, some pieces are more central than others. Scientists don't know which puzzles or pieces are the most important, so they conduct research to find the pieces, put them together, and try to extrapolate information to determine the big picture even when some pieces are still missing. They might follow the scientific method to determine facts about each piece, but on a larger scale, science looks a lot like people trying different experiments and failing many times before they succeed. Neil Gershenfeld, director of MIT's Center for Bits and Atoms, writes that "to find something that's not already on the map, you need to leave the road and wander about in the woods beside it." He feels that nonscientists do not recognize that "science only appears to be goal-directed after the fact. While it's unfolding, it's more like a chaotic dance of improvisation than a victory march."

While the scientific method seems straightforward and nonscientists might think of scientists as superrational, methodological people, science on a broader scale is not always linear. No map or diagram can show the way to prove or disprove a theory. Instead, scientists have to use their creativity to come up with hypotheses, experiments, and analyses.

The solutions to nature's puzzles lead to new understandings of existing theories, form the bases of new theories, and result in new techniques for experimentation. When a puzzle reaches a certain stage, it becomes easier and easier to put in the pieces. The research accelerates. A breakthrough occurs when the pictures on the puzzle become visible—when a central piece is placed that allows whole new areas to emerge. Solving an important puzzle can lead to the start of many other new puzzles.

Of course, because scientists are human, they can discover complex theories while also misinterpreting or imperfectly presenting data. Real science can lead to new theories that are wrong and subsequently disproven. Scientists aren't always right, but that's OK—being wrong is part of the scientific process. The problem is that many people find it very difficult to distinguish disproven theories (based in real science) from made-up science. Whether it leads to correct conclusions or not, real science always follows the scientific method and tests disprovable hypotheses. It also relies on feedback from the scientific community to ensure that it is up to snuff. This often occurs at scientific conferences and through peer-reviewed literature.

PEER-REVIEWED JOURNALS

Prior to the 1600s, scientists privately communicated their findings and ideas in letters, gave public lectures, and wrote books once the experiments were completed and their ideas and theories had matured. There was no way of publishing increments of one's research to demonstrate that one was practicing science properly or invite fellow experts to comment on or even participate in the research. The advent of peer-reviewed scientific journals in 1665 allowed scientists to publish the results of individual experiments as they conducted research. Data would only be published after other scientists reviewed it, and so journals required collaboration and communication among scientists unlike ever before. Science became more accessible, more public, and more democratic, and, as journalist James Somers put it, "scientists from that point forward became like the social insects: They made their progress steadily, as a buzzing mass."

When a group of researchers have completed an experiment or make an interesting discovery, they write a scientific paper about their research and submit it to relevant scientific journals. Upon receiving a manuscript, a staff editor with expertise in the scientific field covered by the paper reads it and decides whether to send the paper for external review or return it to the authors. Most scientific journals use a single-blind, peer-review system to evaluate their manuscripts. This means the editor sends the manuscripts to at least two external peer reviewers who have expertise in the paper's research area. The reviewers act as referees, reading the paper and judging the quality of the work described. In the single-blind process, these referees know who wrote the paper, but the authors never officially find out the identity of the referees.

If referees or editors aren't satisfied with the manuscript, they send it back to the authors to make changes. Then the authors resubmit a revised version of the paper. This back-and-forth can happen several times before the journal accepts the manuscript for publication. Once the manuscript has met the scientific standards of the referees and the editor, the journal publishes the paper, circulating it among the broader scientific community.

Journals are not all equal. *Cell*, *Nature*, and *Science* are some of the most prominent ones, and they only publish the most important papers. Getting a paper published in one of these journals assures the authors of a wide readership and

Part of being a scientist is reading other scientists' work in journals and on preprint servers. The dramatic increase in publications over the past several decades has made it hard for scientists to keep up with all the new findings in their field.

significant prestige, so publication in these journals is highly competitive. *Nature* receives about two hundred manuscripts a week but can publish no more than 8 percent of them, so it must be very selective. This means the papers have withstood rigorous peer review and experts have judged them to be of importance to all scientists. Researchers in all areas of science, from medicine to biology, from physics to mathematics, dream of publishing their work in one of these journals. Every research university in the world has access to these journals, and they are read by many scientists.

Peer review is essentially science's quality control. It has been around for about 350 years. Henry Oldenburg (1618–1677), the editor of the *Philosophical Transactions of the Royal Society*, may have been the first editor to use the system. Since the 1960s the number of journals has ballooned, and the need for impartial experts capable of reviewing scientific manuscripts has grown. Each year about two million papers are published in roughly forty thousand journals. Peer review is done voluntarily, so academics are not paid for the reviews they write. Most scientists see this as pivotal to scientific progress and are willing to volunteer to peer-review.

But the process is imperfect. It takes about five hours to write a review. That means that each year scientists spend about 68.5 million hours reviewing papers without compensation from for-profit publishers. The unpaid cost of peer review in 2008 was estimated to be $3.5 billion. Scientists are writing so many papers that they struggle to find the time to read anybody else's work. Since the end of World War II (1939–1945), the number of papers has doubled about every nine years. This has placed enormous stress on researchers who peer-review the papers. It takes a long time, usually many months, for research to go through peer review and publication. But despite using peer review, scientific journals sometimes publish fraudulent or flawed papers and often turn down papers with innovative ideas. That a paper has been published in a highly selective journal that uses independent reviewers is a good indicator that the authors' work is legitimate and makes a significant contribution to science.

RULE 1

Research published in peer-reviewed journals has undergone rigorous quality control by experts in the field. The most important papers are published in the top peer-reviewed journals: *Science, Nature, Cell, Proceedings of the National Academy of Sciences, Journal of New England Medicine,* and the *Lancet.* If something originates from a peer-reviewed journal, it generally is legitimate.

PREDATORY JOURNALS

Journal articles have become the currency of science. They are used to award funding, tenure, promotions, and job offers in academia. Some universities, and even some countries, give researchers financial bonuses for each paper published. Unfortunately, the emphasis on the number of publications has had some negative consequences. Researchers may submit lower-quality manuscripts and papers with irreproducible results just to increase the length of their résumés.

Some journals do not use peer review. These so-called predatory journals instead charge a price for publication (typically $100 to $2,000). In exchange for the fee, authors can bypass peer review. They might want to do this if they conducted their experiments dishonestly, want to convince consumers about the effectiveness of a product, or otherwise hope to trick readers into thinking the research was legitimate. Predatory journals often have names that sound like scientific journals, such as the *Journal of Integrative Oncology*, and they look just like peer-reviewed journals. The main purpose of predatory journals is to make money for the publishers. As a result, they provide an outlet for unreviewed research and inflate the résumés of unscrupulous researchers. These journals and the papers that they publish can mislead both nonscientists and scientists.

German journalist Svea Eckert and her colleagues examined some of these predatory journals. They found that the majority of the papers published in the journals do come from scientists working at academic institutions, but many others are submitted by medical and biotech companies trying to hype their untested and unproven products. To test the predatory journals' quality control, Eckert wrote a fake article that claimed beeswax was a more effective treatment for cancer than conventionally used chemotherapies. Her paper was accepted and printed by the

Journal of Integrative Oncology. Having proven to herself that it is easy to publish dangerous misinformation that would have been rejected in the first round of peer review, Eckert, along with her colleagues, went on to document how the tobacco company Philip Morris, the pharmaceutical company AstraZeneca, and the nuclear safety company Framatome have used predatory journals to try to make their research seem more legitimate.

Many scientists look upon predatory journals with disdain. Alan Finkel, Australia's former chief scientist, holds the opinion that "if journals are the gatekeepers [of science], then predatory journals are the termites that eat the gates and make the community question the integrity of the structure." Librarian Jeffrey Beall has published a list of nearly twenty-five hundred known predatory journals on his website.

RULE 2

Research published in known predatory journals should be treated with distrust. A list of nearly twenty-five hundred known predatory journals is given at https://beallslist.net/.

PREPRINTS

Preprint servers are online databases where researchers can post manuscripts online before submitting them to peer-reviewed journals. This allows them to provide fellow scientists with a glimpse into current research projects, as well as invite the broader scientific community to do informal external reviews. Preprint servers give free online access to readers who can't afford peer-reviewed journals and release the papers in just a few days rather than months.

HOW TO READ A PEER-REVIEWED SCIENTIFIC ARTICLE

Scientific papers are difficult to read. Scientists have to compress lots of information into a very small space. To be concise and accurate, they use technical jargon. Typically, papers only show a small part of a puzzle in immense detail. To get the big picture, you have to read numerous associated papers. That can take a lot of time, especially if you aren't familiar with all the jargon. However, many of the prestigious journals listed in Rule 1 (page 15) offer brief descriptions, often called "news briefs," of the most important papers. Science journalists employed by the journal write these short descriptions for interested nonexperts. They are from a paragraph to a page long, are written to engage the reader, and can be trusted. Look for one of these summaries if you struggle to understand all the language in the paper itself—it will give you a clear idea of what the paper says. Unfortunately, only the most important publications are summarized in this manner.

Should you want to or have to read a scientific paper, know that most journals require that their articles follow the same distinctive structure. Journal articles start with the title, the names of the authors (who came up with the idea, did the experiments, and wrote the paper), and an abstract. The abstract is a short summary of the research, a single paragraph that is no longer than three hundred words written by the authors themselves. The introduction places the work in context of all the other research that has been done, gives the surrounding history, and justifies the work. The conclusion summarizes the results, often pointing out shortcomings in the research and hinting at future directions for the researchers to take. The middle three sections of the paper—the methods, results, and discussion— are the meat of the paper. They describe how the research was done (methods), present the data obtained (results), and interpret what the results mean (discussion).

In reading a scientific paper, nonscientists should look at the abstract, introduction, and conclusion first, as these sections will cover the reasons that the scientists conducted their research and whether their findings support or disprove their hypothesis. The middle three sections often feature details about measurements, equations, and analysis that might go over a nonexpert's head. But if you want to be a professional scientist, you might find it informative and helpful to look at these sections too, as you one day will write similar papers about your own research.

Many universities and research institutes also publish press releases highlighting research conducted by their faculty. Unlike scientific papers, the aim of these press releases is to enhance the universities' reputations or to attract venture capitalists to fund start-up companies that are based on the research being described. Press releases need to be read with a little more care, as they sometimes contain exaggerations.

The particle size depend___ error in single angle mole___ ___ht measurements can be c___ using Equation 5.[2] This ___ ___on can then be used to c___ ___ the upper size limit for a ___ ___efined acceptable error in t___ ___olecular weight measureme___.

$$\%E_M = |P(\theta) - 1| * 100 \qquad (5)$$

Figure 3 shows a plot of the calculated %Error in molecular weight as a function of particle size for aqueous samples ($\tilde{n}_o = 1.333$) ___aracterized with a single angle

Scientific papers can be difficult to read because they use very precise language and assume readers are familiar with the concepts discussed. But with the knowledge gained here, patience, and techniques such as highlighting, note-taking, and researching unfamiliar language or ideas, a nonscientist can figure out what a scientific paper is saying.

Mathematicians, computer scientists, and physicists have been using preprint servers for decades. The most commonly used server for these scientists is ArXiv, pronounced "archive" (the *X* is the Greek letter "chi"), which opened on August 14, 1991. By the end of 2014 it had more than one million preprints. Preprints are also slowly gaining popularity in the biological sciences, particularly after being endorsed by some major funding agencies and a Nobel Prize–winning scientist. Cold Spring Harbor Laboratory runs the most popular preprint server in the biological sciences, bioRxiv. It was launched as a nonprofit service in 2013. Most servers give each preprint a digital object identifier (DOI) so people can easily find them, time-stamp any revisions so readers know if a preprint has been updated, and allow anyone to read and comment on a preprint.

The COVID-19 pandemic that began in 2019 exposed weaknesses in science's publishing system. During the pandemic, huge numbers of scientists rushed to publish certified science about the coronavirus's spread, effective treatments, and other related research that could help save lives. Peer-reviewed journals tried to keep up. In numerous cases peer-reviewed papers went from submission to online publication in a week or two, but the majority of journals could not cope with the increased submissions. By the end of April 2020, a few months into the pandemic, more than seventy-five hundred COVID-related papers had been published, most of them on preprint servers—meaning they had not undergone the quality control of peer review. Because of the sheer quantity of submissions, the most qualified researchers didn't have time to peer-review papers. Preprint servers should have filled the void, but they were swamped by submissions related to COVID-19. Researchers had a hard time sifting through everything on the servers to identify the most important, accurate science about the coronavirus to use in their own work. Everyone was an expert, everyone wanted a slice of the pie, and no one was doing thorough quality control.

Christian Drosten, director of Germany's Institute of Virology, helped identify the SARS-CoV-1 virus in 2003. During the COVID-19 pandemic, he was Germany's media and government expert on anything related to the SARS-CoV-2 virus. In an interview with the *Guardian*, he said, "In February, there were many interesting preprints around. Now you can read through fifty before you find something that's actually solid and interesting. A lot of research resources are being wasted."

Science doesn't usually offer a quick fix. New technologies and medicines often take years to prove that they are safe and effective. Yet the surging COVID-19 pandemic forced scientists to condense this process to mere months. With people's lives at stake, speed was of the essence. But too many people working quickly on the same project overwhelmed the peer-review

RULE 3

The work on preprint servers has not yet undergone peer review. If you see something that originated from a preprint server, realize that other scientists and journal editors haven't certified it as real, legitimate science yet. Rather, the authors posted it for fellow scientists to evaluate and use as building blocks for their own research. Check how long the work has been on the preprint server. If more than a year has passed, and the work hasn't yet been published in a peer-reviewed journal, be very skeptical of it.

journal system. Researchers were stuck trying to separate good science from unproven junk science. Some didn't even make the effort to read preprints. Preprint servers became littered with immature and unproven science. Fastidious research standards were being sacrificed for speed.

EXAGGERATING SCIENCE

News is all about the exceptional. The more spectacular the science is, the more newsworthy it becomes. Scientists need research grants to fund their work, universities rely on gifts from funders, small start-up companies require investors, and the media wants to woo new readers. Each of these groups has incentives to exaggerate and juice up the science, and unfortunately, that happens all too often.

In 2014 Chris Chambers and his colleagues at Cardiff University conducted a study to establish whether the misreporting observed in the media came from the universities that scientists worked at. Were university press releases exaggerating claims to enhance their reputations? To answer that question, the Chambers team examined all health-related science press releases issued by the top twenty universities in the United Kingdom in 2011, read the associated peer-reviewed articles, and then compared the resultant news stories. They tried to identify who was inserting the embellishments. Did the exaggerations originate in the peer-reviewed articles, the university press release, or the news reports? After reading and analyzing 462 papers, their corresponding press releases, and 668 news reports, the Chambers team concluded that most of the exaggerations originated in the press releases written by the universities, that the news reports carried forward the exaggerations, and that there was no correlation between the extent of the exaggerations and news coverage.

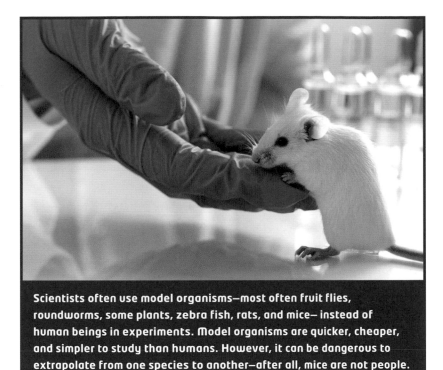

Scientists often use model organisms—most often fruit flies, roundworms, some plants, zebra fish, rats, and mice— instead of human beings in experiments. Model organisms are quicker, cheaper, and simpler to study than humans. However, it can be dangerous to extrapolate from one species to another—after all, mice are not people.

A typical exaggeration they encountered was the suggestion that results had been obtained through research done on humans when they actually came from research on model organisms such as mice. Another favorite was the age-old temptation to imply that correlation implies causation. For example, researchers might find a correlation between red wine consumption and length of life, but that doesn't necessarily mean that drinking red wine is responsible for living longer. It could be that red-wine drinkers are wealthier and have better health care. Even major news outlets are susceptible to this exaggeration. *Time* magazine once ran the headline, "Scientists Say Smelling Farts Might Prevent Cancer," based on a peer-reviewed article that merely pointed out that certain sulfide compounds (sulfur smells like

THE INDUSTRY OF SCIENCE

To be successful in the global market, a country's economy has to grow. Creating new, science-based technologies has become an increasingly popular way for nations to increase their economic strength. Scientists are often eager to guide scientific research out of the laboratory and into the market. While many scientists work in academia or for government organizations, many also do research and develop promising new technologies in the private sector, often for small companies called start-ups. The most successful start-ups are often bought by bigger tech companies, and the scientists go on to work in those larger companies' own research divisions. But the need for growth and profit above all else places pressure on scientists to keep producing results and technologies at higher rates. That can result in corners being cut and results being exaggerated or even fabricated.

A similar problem is present in academia and publicly funded science. Among academics there is a popular saying: "publish or perish." The university research system is built on publishing results in high-impact journals. The rewards for being first to publish new results or getting accepted to *Cell*, *Nature*, or *Science* are substantial, and the penalties for getting it wrong or publishing irreproducible results are minor. So some scientists submit sloppy research for publication before it is ready. Some of this slips through peer-review quality controls.

While many consider science a pursuit of knowledge for its own sake, economic and social forces can influence which science gets published and which scientists get employed and funded. Critically analyze why the science you are reading was published. Are the authors trying to attract investors, sell a product, or enlighten the reader with new information?

rotten eggs) are useful in studying the ways that our cells' mitochondria fail to function properly. The magazine has since issued a corrected title.

Universities and news outlets might exaggerate the findings of real scientific research, but the science in those situations is legitimate. Sometimes, however, what seems like legitimate science is actually fake. If the science sounds too good to be true, is too wacky to be real, or very conveniently supports a contentious cause, then you might want to go to the source of the research. See whether it was published in a peer-reviewed journal and what the original paper actually says. This book will help you recognize fake science, understand where it comes from, and give you the tools you need to detect fake science.

RULE 4

Check that the research was actually done on humans. Just because a certain drug works on rats or mice does not mean it will work in humans.

RULE 5

Correlation does not imply causation. Just because you can see a connection or a mutual relationship between two variables, it doesn't necessarily mean that one causes the other. Other variables might be involved.

2

FAKE SCIENCE

Where real science has been confirmed by experiments, fake science has not. This is often because the results of scientific experiments, recorded in peer-reviewed journals, contradict the fake science, thus proving it wrong. Other times, the decisive experiments haven't been done yet, and the existing "science" is fabricated (as in the case of quackery).

To detect fake science, you must first know what real science is, and then you must know why someone would want to distribute made-up scientific data. Some people and companies use fake science to sell their products. Some want to sway public policy and use pseudoscience to argue for their irrational beliefs about scientific advancements, such as opposition to vaccines and genetically modified foods or advocate for unscientific medical practices, such as homeopathy. Finally, some people use exaggerated, spectacular, and often false scientific results and headlines to lead us to visit their websites so they can earn a few extra bucks off our clicks.

Fake science is a subcategory of fake news, false or misleading information presented as news. Fake news has been around as long as people have been spreading news, but social media gave it legs. The internet has changed the way news and science are communicated. In 1994 there were fewer than three thousand websites. By 2014 there were nearly one billion sites. We have instant access to more news and information than ever before. Facebook and Twitter have unprecedentedly large followings (2.7 billion and 330 million users, respectively) and have the potential to spread information farther and faster than any TV channel or newspaper.

The internet makes it cheap and easy to publish your own website. This has enabled the rise of inexpensive alternatives to the established news sources. Many of these news outlets do not have editorial processes designed to establish the accuracy and credibility of the information they publish. Some intentionally spread false information. These are the fake news outlets. Fake news outlets spread disinformation to influence political policy and debates, sell products and ideas, and deceive readers into clicking on links, thereby maximizing traffic and increasing the profits of the fake news outlets.

More conventional news sites and TV channels can also contribute to the problem of fake news. In the US, CNN and Fox News are the most popular news sources for liberals and conservatives, respectively. Although both are news outlets with big budgets and audiences, they still have a high percentage of misrepresentation of facts. PolitiFact, an independent fact-checking website, has found that 20 percent of CNN assertions were mostly or completely false, and more than half of Fox News's information was incorrect. News outlets often misrepresent science to create controversy, score more viewers, and generate revenue.

RULE 6

Beware of spectacular extraordinary claims. If you find something that makes you gasp and say, "I can't believe that," you probably shouldn't believe it without seeing really reliable proof, such as a peer-reviewed paper. Beware if a piece of news or a social media post stirs up intense feelings, especially outrage. It was most likely designed to short-circuit your critical-thinking skills by playing on your emotions.

Trolls and bots also contribute to the problem. Trolls use social media to confuse complex news stories by adding incorrect facts, release inflammatory statements to start arguments, and strive to polarize debates. Some trolls create automated computer programs called bots, designed to spread disinformation and discord through social media networks. Facebook estimates that as many as sixty million of its users might be bots. These trolls and bots thrive because more than 47 percent of Americans sometimes or often get their news from social media. In the 2016 US presidential election, around 20 percent of all tweets were generated by bots, and a 2018 study published in the *American Journal of*

A protester holds up a sign claiming that the generally reliable British news outlet BBC is "fake news." Fake news came to the forefront of public debate during the US's 2016 presidential elections. Candidate Donald Trump claimed that more liberal-leaning news outlets were fake news, contributing to millions of people turning to outlets and social media that reinforced their biases.

Public Health reported that Russian trolls and sophisticated bot accounts tweeted a plethora of vaccine-related messages. The aim of the tweets was not to influence the vaccine debate, as there were equal numbers of pro- and anti-vaccine tweets. Instead, they were designed to increase the polarization of American society by sending out tweets using divisive language linking vaccination to racial and social disparities.

In March 2018, MIT researchers Soroush Vosoughi, Deb Roy, and Sinan Aral published a paper, "The Spread of True and False News Online," in *Science*. They examined the spread of 126,000 true and false news stories that were tweeted and retweeted by about three million people. The veracity of the news stories was determined by six independent fact-checking organizations, including Snopes, PolitiFact, and FactCheck.org.

The research showed that people are more likely to repeat (in person or on social media) fake science news than real science news.

Imagine you are looking up some information about a common neurological disease. You find fifteen reputable-looking sites. They all have very similar information, except one has a new factoid you haven't seen on any of the other sites. As suggested by the findings of Vosoughi, Roy, and Aral, this is the information you are likely to retweet or pass on to your friends. The fake news is more novel and often evokes more emotion

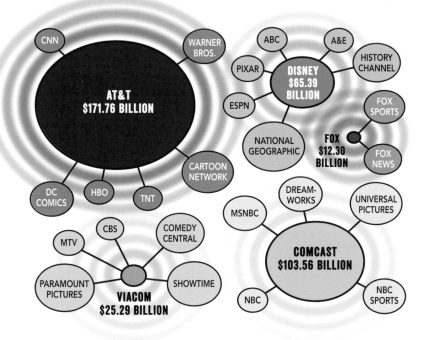

Most news sites and mainstream media channels are owned by a select few parent companies. Tracing sources of ownership and funding can help you determine the biases that might be present in a piece of news.

than the real news. Even the most reliable and steady Twitter users occasionally succumb and retweet false news. These tweets often stand out from all the other tweets sent out in the previous sixty days. Many retweeters pay more attention to whether something is popular than whether its facts are correct. The sheer quantity of information on the internet increases the difficulty in determining what is real and what is fake.

THE INFODEMIC

When SARS-CoV-2, the virus that causes the respiratory illness COVID-19, reared its head in 2019, it was new to science. It had a dramatic effect on all people's lives, and for months, the news reported on study after study about the virus. By the time people had begun to form their opinions on the disease and its spread, scientists hadn't yet had enough time to reach consensus on many aspects of the pandemic. Scientists needed more time to understand the characteristics of its spread. Throughout the pandemic's rampage, many conflicting theories and models appeared. This seeming lack of scientific consensus fertilized the ground for conspiracy theories and false health advice. In mid-February 2020, Tedros Adhanom Ghebreyesus, director-general of the World Health Organization (WHO), warned the Munich Security Conference that "we're not just fighting an epidemic; we're fighting an infodemic. Fake news spreads faster and more easily than the virus, and it is just as dangerous. . . . This is a time for facts, not fear. This is a time for rationality, not rumors. This is a time for solidarity, not stigma."

Manlio De Domenico is the head of the Complex Multilayer Networks Lab at the Bruno Kessler Foundation's Center for Information and Communication Technologies in Trento, Italy. He and his colleagues used machine learning to analyze more than 112 million COVID-related tweets in sixty-four languages.

Waves of unreliable and low-quality information arrived in some countries before the virus did, exposing those places to irrational social behavior and serious public health threats. The level of misinformation rose exponentially and then in most countries fell as the pandemic progressed.

A similar study led by Kathleen Carley, a professor of computer science at Carnegie Mellon University, found that in the two hundred million coronavirus-related tweets that were sent in the first five months of the pandemic, 45 percent were sent by accounts that behaved more like bots than humans. The researchers also found at least one hundred false narratives in the tweets.

Some of the misinformation that bots spread is ridiculous, but some is dangerous. People might spread it to gain political advantage or out of xenophobic spite. In the UK, 5G telephone masts were burned after Facebook and Twitter buzzed with claims that 5G networks were responsible for COVID-19. And in a small Ukrainian town, violence erupted when buses full of Ukrainian evacuees arrived from Wuhan, China, the province where SARS-CoV-2 was first discovered. Others might spread well-intentioned but misguided health advice. That can be just as dangerous as outright bigotry. Hundreds of Iranians died after drinking methanol, believing from misinformation on social media that it would protect them from the virus.

RULE 7

News that is riddled with spelling and grammatical errors is suspect. If the author couldn't be bothered to spell-check it, it likely wasn't fact-checked either.

WHAT IS CLICKBAIT?

The *Oxford English Dictionary* defines *clickbait* as "material put on the internet in order to attract attention and encourage visitors to click on a link to a particular web page." Often the pages will have intriguing, thought-provoking, or controversial images with headlines such as "You won't believe this" or "Find out the whole shocking truth." If you get sucked in, you will click through many pages and advertisements before you find out that the story really isn't very interesting. Clickbait's true purpose is to lure you into the advertisements. It is a game of bait and switch that uses the promise of compelling information to get you to click your way through a website, much akin to the "Breaking News" headlines on TV that keep you watching through the advertisements. The more recent sharebait encourages people to share and repost the headline. Headlines are written so that people will share them without having to read the content.

Be leery of any information you find when following clickbait. It may be funny and shocking, but it is not the place to find real science.

Clickbait often looks like real news, but uses misleading or sensational headlines that encourage you to click on the article. Websites that host clickbait make money off of users' clicks. It's always best to check reputable news outlets because they use editors who check the veracity of the story.

THE ORIGINS OF FAKE SCIENCE

In 1761 John Hill published "Cautions against the Immoderate Use of Snuff." In this paper he linked the tobacco found in snuff to lip, mouth, and throat cancer. The ideas and thoughts he expressed in the pamphlet were correct, but it would take a few hundred years for the public and the government to accept his findings.

Fourteen years after Hill described the link between tobacco and throat cancer, Percivall Pott, a surgeon at St. Bartholomew's Hospital in London, noted that chimney sweeps had an excessively high rate of scrotal cancer. He attributed the formation of the scrotal cancer to exposure to soot. Hill and Pott were among the first to identify carcinogens, or cancer-causing substances. During Pott's lifetime, children as young as five years old were apprenticed as chimney sweeps. Pott died the same year that the British Parliament's Chimney Sweepers Act 1788 was passed thanks in part to his advocacy about the dangers of the job. The act forbade master sweeps from having apprentices younger than eight years old. It took a few decades after Pott's manuscript was published for chimney sweeps to become aware of the dangers of soot and learn how to avoid it, especially in their scrotal areas. Once this knowledge caught on, the incidence of scrotal cancer for chimney sweeps decreased. Unfortunately, the same did not occur in response to Hill's work. Centuries after he proved the link between tobacco use and cancer, public health professionals are still trying to combat lung cancer by reducing smoking. Why is that?

"Doubt is our product," a tobacco company executive wrote in 1969 in an internal memo. To undermine scientific research that indicated a link between nicotine and lung cancer, the tobacco industry systematically challenged

Be Happy - Go Lucky!

An old advertisement for cigarettes lacks warnings about health risks. The tobacco lobby so thoroughly discredited Hill's 1761 research linking cancer to smoking that it wouldn't be until 1964, over two hundred years later, that the US government recognized the link.

Dorothy Collins, "The Sweetheart of Lucky Strike"

LUCKIES TASTE BETTER THAN ANY OTHER CIGARETTE !
Fine tobacco—and only fine tobacco—can give you the perfect mildness and rich taste you get in a Lucky Strike!

L.S./M.F.T.- Lucky Strike Means Fine Tobacco

scientific evidence and the way science was done. It sought to cast doubt in consumers by using sophisticated public relations approaches to distort the science that proved smoking was carcinogenic. Together with a team of advertising agencies and lobbyists, the tobacco companies convinced some politicians and journalists to accept that all science, particularly research surrounding tobacco, was never 100 percent certain, that journalists always needed to present a "balanced" perspective with views from both sides of an issue to be objective, and that inaction was the wisest response to uncertainty.

In the twenty-first century, most people do believe there is a link between tobacco smoking and lung cancer, but the damage to science's public image has already been done.

Large segments of the general public are skeptical of science. Journalists, trying to be impartial and objective, still present many different opinions even when the science clearly backs one side of an issue over the other. The tobacco lobby's tactics are still used by other groups that want to dispute scientific evidence, such as anti-vaccine groups and climate change deniers. The tobacco industry continues to use these strategies with the advent of vapes and electronic cigarettes as a "healthier" alternative to smoking.

In his article "Consilience and Consensus," science writer and historian Michael Shermer describes why scientific theories are an easy target for these campaigns. All scientific theories start out as an idea proposed and believed by a small minority of scientists. If the theory is valid and robust, the evidence collected from multiple lines of research all lead to the same conclusion, and eventually the majority of scientists accept the theory as scientific truth. Scientists have long reached consensus about the tobacco-cancer link, climate change, and the effectiveness of vaccination. But skeptics and industries with a vested interest (such as tobacco and fossil fuel companies) have attacked many strands of research claiming that consensus hasn't been attained yet. They don't have to disprove the theory by undermining the consensus. All they need to do is find some experiments that are easy to manipulate, weak, controversial, or hard to understand, and pick on them. Even if hundreds or thousands of experiments strongly support the theory, the deniers can rely on journalists to give equal exposure to shaky, uncertain research and the more robust research. By focusing on the weakest link, the deniers instill doubt.

To illustrate how deniers do this, think of climate change research as solving a massive puzzle with 10,000 pieces, of which 9,998 pieces have been placed in their correct positions. In a five-minute TV segment, the climate researchers get to describe that they have read all the research (the 9,998 puzzle pieces), that they have spent decades studying the problem, and that they see how the pieces all fit together. In the following five minutes, a climate change denier describes in excruciating detail how two pieces are missing and how important these two pieces are to the picture. Because climate change is so complicated, ordinary viewers of this program can't read all the research, can't see the big picture in the same way as the experts, and may start doubting the science although consensus has been reached. When news outlets give equal airtime to scientific consensus and fringe, often unsupported views, this is called false balance.

This strategy of producing doubt to undercut public health efforts and regulatory interventions designed to reduce the harms of smoking ended up damaging all of science. Public trust in science and the scientific process was the collateral damage of these campaigns.

RULE 8

Although a political debate requires two opposing sides, a scientific consensus does not. Beware of "false balance," in which media outlets give equal time to both a scientific consensus and the fringe science or opinions that disagree with the consensus. Beware of people expressing rogue views that are funded by companies that have something to gain from undermining scientific consensus and sowing distrust in science.

THE DIFFICULTIES IN SEPARATING REAL SCIENCE FROM FAKE SCIENCE

The complexity and sheer volume of scientific knowledge is part of the reason the tobacco industry, climate change deniers, and others can undermine science. Our scientific knowledge is rapidly increasing. This is great, because we know more and more about the workings of the world around us. Scientists have found ways for us to live longer, become more energy efficient, and live more comfortable lives. But we have long passed the point where any one person is capable of understanding all of science.

At the same time that the amount of scientific knowledge in the world increases, the rate of increase also grows. Scientific insights and technological advancements are growing exponentially, while the structures of our society, such as government, education, and economy, are designed for predictable, linear increases. This disparity can lead to problems. And science is becoming more complex thanks to a spike in interdisciplinary work between previously disparate fields. The increase in complexity has resulted in an ever-widening gap between the scientific knowledge of students, legislators, religious leaders, and voters and the total available science knowledge. It has also inadvertently facilitated the growth of fake science.

Now that we know the complexity of science makes it hard to distinguish between real and fake science, let's see how the brain has conspired to make it so hard for us to detect fake science.

COGNITIVE BIASES
NEGATIVITY BIAS

It normally takes a fraction of a second for the body to react to visual information. But that might not be fast enough if you

LINEAR VS. EXPONENTIAL GROWTH

Many natural phenomena have approximately linear growth rates. A tree grows at pretty much the same rate throughout its life—it doesn't grow faster and faster as it gets older. While it might grow faster in the summer than in the winter, on average it grows at the same speed. Linear growth occurs when the thing being measured is independent: what is happening to one tree has little to no effect on whether it will happen to another tree. Exponential growth occurs when the growth rate itself gets quicker with time. An infectious disease outbreak is an example of a natural phenomenon with an exponential growth rate. Initially a small number of patients spread the disease to only a few other people, but with time, the number of patients increases dramatically. The more people have been infected, the faster the disease spreads to more people, because all of the infected people can transmit the disease to many others. Researchers observe exponential growth less frequently than linear growth because rapid exponential growth quickly reaches an upper limit and stops. In the example of disease spread, the upper limit is the total population of people. Eventually, the disease will run out of people to infect.

People often underestimate exponential growth rates because they are counterintuitive and rare. Unless researchers observing these trends are vigilant, their visual systems will trick them, and they will interpret an exponential growth pattern in its early progression as a linear growth pattern. Such mistakes lead to many errors in science reporting.

are in immediate danger. Suppose you see a poisonous snake that's coiled up and ready to strike. It could spring up and bite you faster than your brain processes the image from your eyes. So the brain has a built-in shortcut. When people encounter a danger such as a deadly snake, their heartbeat increases, their blood pressure rises, certain hormones surge through their body, and their blood sugar level rises—all in much less than half a second. These reactions give their body the energy it needs to either fight or flee the danger, even before their brain has fully registered the image of the threat. Our brains are hardwired to respond to danger.

This ability to evade snakes, lions, scorpions, and other predators has a drawback that makes us susceptible to fake science. We have what psychologists call a negativity bias: our brains respond more vigorously to negative events than positive ones. This bias probably comes from evolution: having a fear response and paying attention to negative stimuli would help ancient humans survive, while too little fear could get them killed. Studies show that people are more likely to remember traumatic incidents. We learn more from failure than success and tend to make more decisions based on negative data than positive data. We are also more likely to perceive negative news as true.

AVAILABILITY BIAS

Our view of the world is skewed by our past experiences. We give our own memories and experiences—and the information available through them—more credence than they deserve. This availability bias is very useful in situations in which we have to make quick decisions and don't have time to critically analyze lots of data, but it messes with our fact-checking skills. We overestimate the likelihood of occurrences that are lodged in our memories, while more likely (but perhaps more boring) explanations only come to mind after conscientious scrutiny. Combined with sensationalizing in news reporting and the lack of access to scientific information, the vivid and novel news stories become what is most available to us. In the fight for neural attention, sensational statements beat out unexciting facts and everyday reality.

CONFIRMATION BIAS

Confirmation bias describes our preference for information that reaffirms the ideas we believe are true. That is why we favor, interpret, and recall information that supports our prior beliefs and values, and why it's hard to change our minds. It is no fun being wrong, and it is not easy to have beliefs that are different from those commonly accepted. Even in science, following the crowd is much easier than finding your own new path. Mostly, that's good, because accepted science is normally right. However, the confirmation bias also leads to overconfidence and poor judgment, and can get in the way of overturning entrenched—but false—ideas. Confirmation bias is wishful thinking and leads to self-deception. It occurs not just in fact-checking but in science itself, where scientists may make errors by reporting and collecting data that supports their ideas, while ignoring or undervaluing results that don't agree with their current theories.

For centuries, European scientists and philosophers believed the sun circled Earth. Around 1514 Polish astronomer Nicolaus Copernicus (1473–1543) proposed that Earth was a planet that orbited the sun. He published his theory in 1543, shortly before his death. The Copernican view of the solar system wasn't globally accepted until the eighteenth century, after Galileo, the astronomer Johannes Kepler (1571–1630), and Newton added their research. Scientists and the general public hadn't accepted the experimental data earlier, because they had to overcome, among other things, their confirmation bias, not because it was difficult to understand or because the experimental evidence was difficult to gather.

Our rational minds are not critical enough to always identify fake science. They need to be trained to overcome cognitive biases—and the purveyors of fake news, who know

RULE 9

Beware of cognitive biases, such as your own negativity, availability, and confirmation biases.

our weaknesses and try to take advantage of them. We have to learn to recognize fake science and not fall for its novelty. In the next few chapters, we will see how to detect science misrepresented for political gain and quackery.

3

THIS IS SCIENCE, NOT POLITICS

Only two scientists and eleven engineers were in the 116th Congress of the United States (2019–2021), while there were 192 lawyers. The seven radio talk show hosts, twenty-seven farmers, and six professional athletes all outnumbered the scientists as well. Similar low numbers are found in Australia and Canada, where scientists make up just 4 percent of parliament. The vast predominance of lawyers in the House of Representatives and the Senate sets the tone for debate in the US Congress. Lawyers seek to win debates, so they use facts selectively and they aren't necessarily looking for the truth, nor are they interested in presenting the whole picture. In contrast, science relies on gathering evidence, weighing that evidence, and validating theories. Scientists and science in general don't do well in politics (Angela Merkel and Margaret Thatcher, both chemists, are obvious exceptions). Scientists believe in the importance of facts and think they can win public debates by using them, despite studies that suggest passionate opinion will often overcome scientific facts, particularly when the opinion is tied to a political identity.

Unfortunately, politicians often play fast and loose with scientific facts to win arguments and votes. They know that people have very strong beliefs, identities, or biases and use that to their advantage. These can be strong enough to override rational analysis in even the most sophisticated scientists. For example, despite having all the facts, training, background knowledge, and scientific competence, both scientists and nonscientists took a long time to acknowledge that Earth was round and that it rotated around the sun. Contemporaries of Charles Darwin (1809–1882) had the scientific chops to understand his theory of evolution, but their religious beliefs were so ingrained that they were not able to accept it. Even that women and men are equally capable as scientists remains more contentious in public opinion than it should be.

Climate change, the safety of vaccinations, and the safety of genetically modified foods are among the latest topics of intense public debate. Because of the confirmation bias, the huge numbers of fake news stories, and their own political and cultural identities, a substantial number of people do not believe in proven science, particularly the science associated with these subjects.

THE POLITICS OF A PANDEMIC

The responses to the COVID-19 pandemic are one example of how political identities define our beliefs. In May 2020, 82 percent of Democrats believed that the coronavirus outbreak was a major threat to the health of the US population. In comparison, only 43 percent of Republicans felt that way. Part of the reason for this difference was that at the time of polling, scientists didn't know enough to predict exactly how bad the pandemic would be. Another reason is that people naturally have different perspectives on issues: someone's "bad" may be someone else's "not so bad."

Many conservatives were deeply disturbed by the infringement of anti-COVID measures, such as wearing face masks and practicing social distancing, into their personal liberties and the economy. Liberals were more willing to accept a massive economic toll if it meant improving public health. Given the lack of consensus among scientists and health professionals early on in the pandemic, politicians molded scientific data to fit their views. Consequently, states with Democratic leadership took a much slower and more cautious approach to relaxing COVID-19 regulations than Republican-led states.

Adhering to mask-wearing and social distancing rules for prolonged periods can be difficult, and you can't touch, taste, feel, or see the benefits. If all of your actions to prevent illness work, the outcome is that you don't get sick. But not being sick was the state you were in before you took those actions. Scientists call this the "prevention paradox." Because of this paradox, some people have a hard time believing that these prevention measures are actually necessary. Their interpretation of the success of social distancing is influenced by their prior beliefs. Some might believe that the prevention measures work and that is why they aren't sick, while others believe that they don't get sick because they do nothing different.

RULE 10

If you read or see something that is very compelling and confirms everything you already believe, make sure the information is coming from a source that is nonpartisan (not affiliated with a political party or identity) and that it doesn't play on a political bias or social identity of yours.

CLIMATE CHANGE

In 1824 French mathematician Joseph Fourier (1768–1830) proposed a radically new theory, the greenhouse effect. He suggested that gases in the atmosphere naturally trap heat on Earth in the same way that a pane of glass keeps heat inside a greenhouse. Scientific research has since proven that he was right. Without atmospheric gases trapping the infrared radiation in Earth's atmosphere, the average temperature of Earth would be −0.4°F (−18°C). All water would be frozen, and no life would be on Earth. The greenhouse effect warms Earth to an average of 59°F (15°C), which allows a variety of life-forms to survive. Fourier was also one of the first scientists to point out that human activity will change the amount of thermal radiation (heat) trapped in the atmosphere, leading to climate change.

About seventy years after Fourier proposed the greenhouse effect, Swedish chemist Svante Arrhenius (1859–1927) published an article, "On the Influence of Carbonic Acid [Carbon Dioxide] in the Air upon the Temperature of the Ground," in which he described how carbon dioxide in the atmosphere traps Earth's heat. He also accurately calculated the temperature increases caused over time by the rise in

GREENHOUSE CULPRITS

Carbon dioxide is a colorless, odorless, and nontoxic gas. It is difficult to visualize and easy to ignore—not ideal properties for a great villain. Politicians who want to help mitigate the effects of climate change have struggled to drum up support for the regulation of this by-product of combustion. A smelly, acrid gas might have been much easier to regulate.

Methane is another greenhouse gas contributing to climate change. It is thirty times more effective at absorbing infrared radiation than the same mass of carbon dioxide. Yet methane currently causes only about one-sixth to one-third the amount of global warming that carbon dioxide does because humans and animals produce less of it.

One of the most potent greenhouse gases is nitrous oxide, which is mainly formed by agricultural activities. It is also commonly known as laughing gas. Nitrous oxide is almost three hundred times more effective at trapping heat than carbon dioxide. Fortunately, human activities don't release nearly as much nitrous oxide as carbon dioxide or methane, and nitrous oxide accounts for less than 10 percent of the greenhouse gas emissions contributing to climate change.

carbon dioxide in the atmosphere. From these calculations, he concluded that Earth's glacial periods, when large parts of the planet were covered with thick sheets of ice, were caused by a reduction in the amount of carbon dioxide in the air. Modern scientists agree. They are concerned because carbon dioxide and other so-called greenhouse gases in Earth's atmosphere are increasing in concentration as a result of human activities. As a consequence, the average temperature of Earth is increasing beyond 59°F (15°C).

The National Aeronautics and Space Administration (NASA) has kept track of this increase using monthly analyses of global temperatures. Researchers assemble the data from various sources, including sixty-three hundred meteorological stations around the world, ship- and buoy-based instruments measuring sea-surface temperatures, and Antarctic research stations. Sixteen of the seventeen warmest years on record have occurred since 2001. (The other was 1998.) The years 2016 and 2020 are tied for the hottest global average temperature—1.7°F (0.9°C) higher than the twentieth century's average temperature—in recorded history. This high temperature was largely due to increases in carbon dioxide and methane levels.

The average global temperature on Earth has increased by about 1.8°F (1.0°C) since 1880, the year the International Meteorological Organization began standardizing the recording of global temperatures. Two-thirds of that warming has occurred since 1975, at a rate of roughly 0.27°F to 0.36°F (0.15°C to 0.20°C) per decade.

On June 23, 1988, James Hansen, then director of NASA's Institute for Space Studies, testified before the US Senate Energy and Natural Resources Committee that "global warming has reached a level such that we can ascribe with a high degree of confidence a cause-and-effect relationship between the greenhouse effect and observed warming. . . . In my opinion, the greenhouse effect has been detected, and it is changing our climate now." Since then, the effect has only become more pronounced.

The North and South Poles have experienced the largest temperature increases. The warming has led to significant melting of sea ice. Perennial, or year-round, sea ice in the Arctic is declining by 9 percent per decade. Long-term temperature forecasts predict a rise of 2.5°F to 10°F (1.4°C to 5.6°C) over

2013 Temperature Anomaly

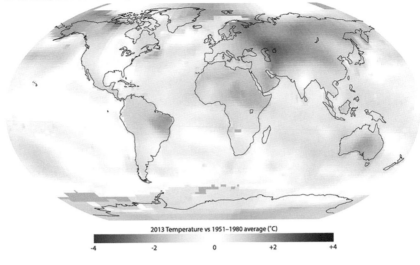

2013 Temperature vs 1951–1980 average (°C)

-4   -2   0   +2   +4

1950–2013 Temperature Trend

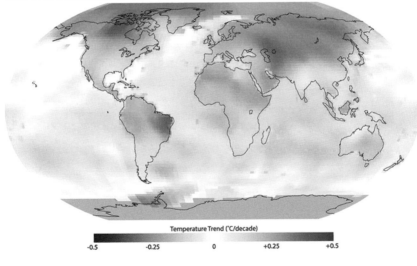

Temperature Trend (°C/decade)

-0.5   -0.25   0   +0.25   +0.5

In the NASA diagram above, the top map shows how the global temperatures in 2013 compared to the average temperatures of the years 1950—1980, where the more orange a region is, the higher the temperature was in 2013. The bottom map shows explicitly how much the temperature has increased since 1950. Both maps demonstrate that global temperatures have risen since 1950.

THIS IS SCIENCE, NOT POLITICS

the next century. This may seem like a small temperature change, but a one- to two-degree drop was all it took to move Earth into the Little Ice Age that occurred seven hundred years ago. These small global changes can have significant local effects. As temperatures warm, glaciers shrink, ice on rivers and lakes breaks up earlier in the season, plant and animal ranges shift, and trees flower sooner each year. The melting of sea ice results in an accelerated global rise in sea levels. Heat waves are longer and more intense. Scientists have shown that climate change is associated with an increase in extreme weather events. Most, but not all, of these events are due to temperature increases.

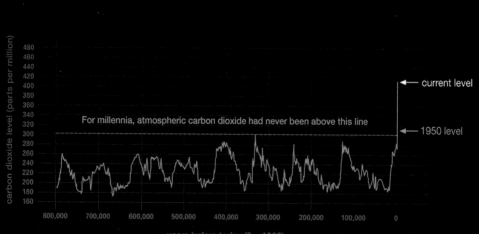

NASA data has recorded the atmospheric carbon dioxide levels from hundreds of thousands of years ago until now. As the graph above shows, these levels only exceeded about 300 parts per million after 1950. Increases in fossil fuel combustion, human and livestock respiration, and cement production have led to this increase.

The National Oceanic and Atmospheric Administration (NOAA) has recorded the number and the cost of all weather-related disasters that have occurred in the United States since 1980. The 1980–2016 annual average was 5.5 events per year. Due to climate change, it increased to 10.6 events for 2012–2016. As the frequency and intensity of extreme weather events increase, so do the costs associated with them. From 1980 to 2020, NOAA recorded 290 weather disasters that have cost more than $1 billion each. The total cost of the events exceeded $1.9 trillion.

POLITICIZATION

One common belief is that the more science knowledge a person has, the more that person supports science. This belief has been borne out by a number of studies, and some Pew Research Center surveys conducted prior to 2016 support that theory. However, a 2016 opinion poll found that this theory is not always valid. When Republicans were asked whether climate change was due to human activity, 19 percent of those with low science knowledge, 25 percent with medium science background, and only 23 percent with high science knowledge agreed there was a link. Well-educated Republicans with an extensive science background were just as likely to have no confidence in climate science as Republicans without science knowledge. But Democrats with an average-to-better scientific understanding are more likely to acknowledge that climate change is linked to human activity than those with a lower understanding of scientific issues. The numbers range from 49 percent for those with low scientific understanding to 93 percent for those with a high science background. The poll also found that people who deeply care about climate change are more likely to know that carbon dioxide is produced as a

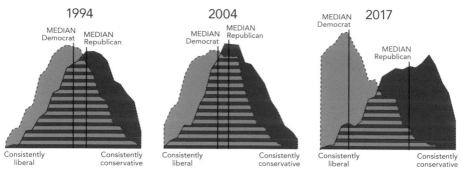

GROWING PARTISAN DIVIDE IN THE UNITED STATES

1994

MEDIAN Democrat
MEDIAN Republican

Consistently liberal — Consistently conservative

2004

MEDIAN Democrat
MEDIAN Republican

Consistently liberal — Consistently conservative

2017

MEDIAN Democrat
MEDIAN Republican

Consistently liberal — Consistently conservative

Source: "The Partisan Divide on Political Values Grows Even Wider," Pew Research Center, October 5, 2017,
https://www.pewresearch.org/politics/2017/10/05/1-partisan-divides-over-political-values-widen/.

The graphs above show distributions of how liberally or conservatively Democrats and Republicans responded to a set of ten political values questions, as surveyed by the Pew Research Center. As years go by, more Democrats answer more liberally, and more Republicans answer more conservatively.

consequence of burning fossil fuels (75 versus 65 percent).

A 2018 Gallup poll confirmed the Pew survey results, showing the party divide. They found that 91 percent of Democrats say they worry a great deal or a fair amount about climate change, while only 33 percent of Republicans say so. Our scientific beliefs seem linked to our political affiliation. For Republicans, climate change denial is a sign, a social cue, that demonstrates membership in the group. Studies show that humans like to stick to their group identifiers.

A Pew poll taken in 2014 compared the opinions of a random sample of the general public with a representative sample of scientists connected to the American Association for the Advancement of Science. One of the largest disconnects between scientists and nonscientists was recorded when they were asked whether they believed that "the earth is getting warmer due to human activity." There was a 37 percent gap between scientists, 87 percent of whom answered yes, and nonscientists, only 50 percent of whom thought that climate change was due to human activity. The gap is even larger if one considers just climate scientists, 97 percent of whom agree that global warming is caused by humans.

Belief in human-caused climate can also be fickle. A University of New Hampshire survey of political independents found that 70 percent believed that human activity caused climate change on a very hot day, but that number fell to 40 percent on very cold days.

Climate skepticism is mainly limited to English-speaking countries. James Painter, a research associate at Reuters Institute, looked at more than two thousand articles and found that "more than 80 percent" of the climate skeptics were found in articles from the US and the UK, compared with articles from Brazil, China, India, and France. Most of the climate change denial occurred in more conservative-leaning newspapers and television stations. And most English-speaking media outlets are guilty of false balance.

In China (the largest producer of carbon dioxide in the world) the media and government move in lockstep, and since the Chinese government has long accepted the link between global warming and human activity, the media fairly represent climate scientists. Although China is the largest producer of carbon dioxide in the world, it is not the largest producer of carbon dioxide *per person* in the world. On that measure, the United States ranks thirteenth in the world, while China is thirty-seventh. This distinction is important because populations vary so drastically between nations, including between the US (about 300 million people) and China (almost 1.5 billion). Hans Rosling, a global health expert and one of the authors of *Factfulness: Ten Reasons We're Wrong about the*

World—and Why Things Are Better Than You Think, says that comparing total carbon dioxide production by nation is a bit like "claiming that obesity [is] worse in China than in the United States because the total bodyweight of the Chinese population [is] higher than that of the US population. Arguing about emissions per nation is pointless when there [is] such enormous variation in population size."

Thirty years ago, when Hansen testified that human activity was responsible for climate change, the impact was dramatic. Newspapers, TV stations, politicians, corporations, and nongovernmental organizations recognized the importance of the problem, and climate change discussions were largely nonpartisan. Since his announcement, scientific certainty that human causes are responsible for climate change has become stronger. As predicted, more wildfires in the western United States, more flooding associated with hurricanes in the southeastern United States, rising sea levels, bleaching of corals, spreading of tropical diseases, and increased ocean acidification have all occurred, yet the US response to the crisis has been lackluster. Congress has had more than six hundred hearings on climate change, but little progress has been made. Meanwhile, concern about climate change has decreased among Republicans. Why? Because in 1989, the fossil fuel industry took a page out of the tobacco industry's playbook and started the anti-science Global Climate Coalition, which began a well-financed campaign to undermine climate science research by polarizing public opinion, creating misinformation, and promoting uncertainty. After the Global Climate Coalition's dissolution in 2001, other propaganda groups took on the same role in promoting anti-science agendas.

Fossil fuel companies have also funded many members of Congress, who go on to debate the facts in campaign

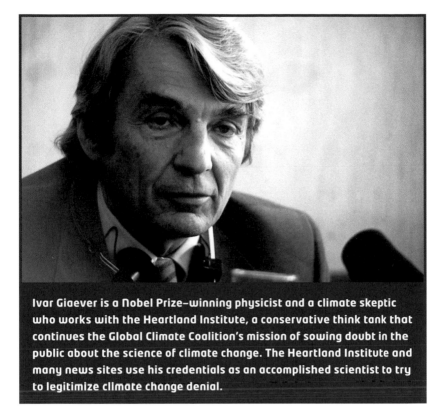

Ivar Giaever is a Nobel Prize–winning physicist and a climate skeptic who works with the Heartland Institute, a conservative think tank that continues the Global Climate Coalition's mission of sowing doubt in the public about the science of climate change. The Heartland Institute and many news sites use his credentials as an accomplished scientist to try to legitimize climate change denial.

speeches, congressional hearings, and committee meetings. By spending years arguing against sound science on a public platform, these politicians have caused voters to lose confidence in the science behind climate change. Kate Marvel, a climate scientist at Columbia University and NASA's Goddard Institute for Space Studies, refuses to debate science in public, especially climate science. In her opinion, "Once you put facts about the world up for debate, you've already lost. Science isn't a popularity contest; if it were, I'd definitely vote to eliminate quantum mechanics, set π to 1, and put radium back in toothpaste." Climate change and the science behind it are fact, not opinion. They are not something we can "agree to disagree" about.

RULE 11

Politicians don't always tell the truth. Sometimes their knowledge of science lets them down, sometimes they follow a misguided party line, and sometimes they have a vested interest in spreading disinformation or obscuring part of the facts.

FIXING THE PROBLEM

Attribution science, which links extreme weather events to climate change, might be the game changer scientists are all hoping for, bringing public opinion in line with climate science. Friederike Otto, a climate modeler at the University of Oxford, uses weather@home, a distributed computing framework that relies on citizen scientists (volunteers who aren't professional scientists) to donate their home computers' idle time so she can perform her attribution calculations. The weather@home project, with Germany's national weather agency, seeks to identify whether a climate event was caused by climate change. Quickly establishing a link between a climate event and climate change, or ruling it out, will be very effective in illustrating the impact human-emitted greenhouse gases have on the weather. Otto says, "If we scientists don't say anything, other people will answer [the question as to whether climate change is real] not based on scientific evidence, but on whatever their agenda is. So, if we want science to be part of the discussion that is happening, we need to say something fast."

After nearly a decade of research and more than 170 research papers, attribution science has matured enough that it is going public. In some cases, because of the advances made

Intense wildfires have become a regular occurrence in the western United States. Increasing global temperatures lead to worse drought conditions in already dry areas, resulting in more frequent and stronger fires. Attribution science is one field that may help determine the extent to which climate change influences wildfires and convince more people that climate change is real and needs solving.

by attribution science, future weather forecasts will be able to show how much more likely an extreme weather event was due to the greenhouse gases released by humans' industrial activities. *Nature* magazine reviewed all the climate attribution studies from 2004 to mid-2018, finding that two-thirds of the climate events examined were more severe due to the release of greenhouse gases from human activities. Of these events, 43 percent were heat events, 18 percent were droughts, and 17 percent were extreme rain or flooding. Attribution studies showed that the 2016 heat waves in Asia, the global heat record in 2016, and the increased ocean temperatures in the Gulf of Alaska and the Bering Sea in 2014–2016 would not have occurred without anthropogenic (human-caused) climate change.

Our current economies of expansion and growth generate too much waste. Plastic items have been found in the deepest trenches of our oceans and in the stomachs of whales, dolphins, and turtles. The photos and videos of plastic pollution go viral online and evoke a visceral feeling of despair and disgust. Due to consumer demands for more ethical and sustainable materials that don't harm the environment, many companies are shifting away from using plastic. Reducing the amount of carbon dioxide and methane released into the atmosphere is a much more difficult task. The only way this can be done is by making changes across all realms: individuals' private choices, public policy, local initiatives, shifts away from economies of growth and expansion, and global agreements. Maintaining and bolstering trust in science has never been more critical.

ANTI-VAXXERS

The vaccination debate is very similar to the one about climate change. In both cases the science is conclusive and the denialists are strongly influenced by their group identity. Fortunately, anti-vaccinators, or anti-vaxxers for short, are not as common as climate change deniers, and neither of the two major political parties in the United States actively opposes vaccination. Anti-vaxxers tend to be on both ends of the political spectrum and are often religious groups, greens (whose political ideology aims to foster an ecologically sustainable society), or libertarians who object that the state has the right to restrict individual liberty so as to promote welfare for all. They distrust pharmaceutical companies and think that money corrupts medicine.

Anti-vaxxers have been around since the first vaccines. In England, in his 1772 sermon, "The Dangerous and Sinful Practice of Inoculation," the Reverend Edmund Massey called vaccination "a diabolical operation." Since then the opposition to vaccination has never completely disappeared.

Acceptance of vaccinations is very important, because vaccination rates of 95 to 99 percent of the population are required to preserve herd immunity against highly contagious diseases, such as measles and chicken pox. Herd immunity allows people who can't receive vaccines (such as young babies) to be protected from deadly illnesses. Vaccinations have helped decrease the prevalence of childhood diseases and have eliminated or nearly eliminated smallpox and polio. However, distrust of vaccinations may undo much of this progress, resulting in outbreaks of previously rare or nonexistent diseases and endangering people who have medical conditions that prevent them from being vaccinated.

THE RISE IN ANTI-VACCINATION

In February 1998 the *Lancet*, a well-respected peer-reviewed medical journal, published an article that reported a connection between the measles, mumps, and rubella vaccine (MMR) and autism in children. The work was done and reported by Andrew Wakefield, a gastroenterologist at the Royal Free Hospital in London. At the time, not much was known about the causes of autism, and the Wakefield paper caused a sensation. Many parents of autistic children came forward to confirm that they first noticed the symptoms of autism in their children shortly after the children had been inoculated with the MMR. The medical community was less impressed because the study only involved eight children, and they knew that children, vaccinated or not, exhibit the first characteristics of autism at

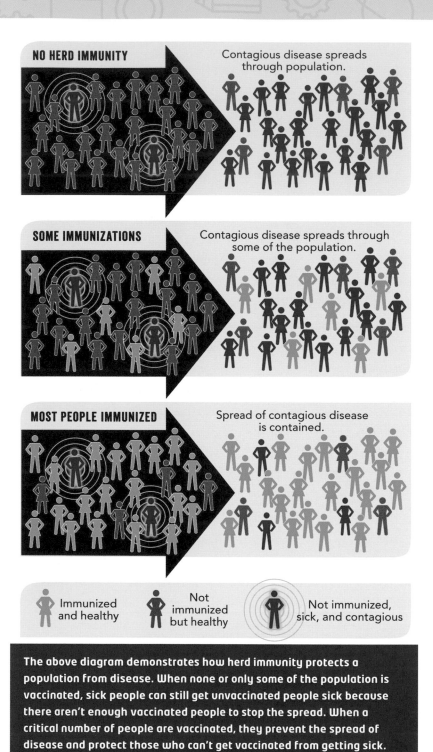

NO HERD IMMUNITY

Contagious disease spreads through population.

SOME IMMUNIZATIONS

Contagious disease spreads through some of the population.

MOST PEOPLE IMMUNIZED

Spread of contagious disease is contained.

Immunized and healthy

Not immunized but healthy

Not immunized, sick, and contagious

The above diagram demonstrates how herd immunity protects a population from disease. When none or only some of the population is vaccinated, sick people can still get unvaccinated people sick because there aren't enough vaccinated people to stop the spread. When a critical number of people are vaccinated, they prevent the spread of disease and protect those who can't get vaccinated from getting sick.

SCIENCE AND THE SKEPTIC

about the age they would normally get the MMR shot. The government tasked the British Medical Research Council to find out if there was any validity to the findings. The council found none, and a number of other papers have been published refuting the findings.

Wakefield vocally and very publicly defended his conclusions and claimed there was a conspiracy to silence him. Journalists covering the controversy found that his continued research was being funded by a group of lawyers, the Legal Aid Board, who were suing the manufacturers of the MMR. Wakefield hadn't disclosed his funding source to anyone, including his coworkers. Ultimately, Wakefield was struck off the medical register and forbidden from practicing medicine in Britain. The *Lancet* retracted his paper, saying it was "utterly false." But the damage was done.

The media grabbed hold of the story, and his ideas attracted many followers, including a number of high-profile celebrities. Actor Jenny McCarthy was particularly taken by Wakefield's story. She has an autistic son, Evan, and is convinced it was the MMR shot that "gave" him autism. In 2007 she went on *The Oprah Winfrey Show* and told the show's millions of viewers about the "dangers" of vaccinations. In the days after the show, she also appeared on *Larry King Live* and *Good Morning America*. In *The Panic Virus*, journalist Seth Mnookin estimates that McCarthy's anti-vaccine message reached fifteen to twenty million people through those shows. Even though celebrities may not be the initial source of scientific information, their words and ideas get spread disproportionately because they are so revered by the general public. A joint study conducted by Oxford University and the Reuters Institute on misinformation related to the COVID-19 pandemic found that 59 percent of the falsehoods involved various forms of reconfiguration, where existing and often true information was spun, twisted, recontextualized, or reworked. Only 38 percent was completely fabricated. Top-down misinformation from politicians, celebrities, and other prominent public figures made up just 20 percent of the claims but accounted for 69 percent of total social media engagement.

After being disgraced in the United Kingdom, Wakefield moved to Austin, Texas, and founded the Autism Media Channel, which makes videos asserting a link between autism and the MMR vaccine. He has also spoken to crowds of supporters of then president Donald Trump to spread his message.

RULE 12

Beware of medical products and scientific ideas promoted by celebrities.

THE CONSEQUENCES OF ANTI-VACCINATION

According to the WHO, a decrease in MMR in Europe, attributed to the Wakefield paper and anti-vaxxer movement, resulted in a fourfold increase in measles in Europe in 2017. "Over 20,000 cases of measles, and 35 lives lost in 2017 alone, are a tragedy we simply cannot accept," said Zsuzsanna Jakab, the WHO regional director for Europe, at the time.

All fifty states in the United States require students to be vaccinated before they enter school. Every state also allows medical exemptions for children whose medical conditions prevent them from being vaccinated. These children are protected from contagious diseases by herd immunity. Since all their classmates are vaccinated, there will be no disease outbreaks and no danger for them to catch a preventable disease. Fifteen states allow parents to forgo vaccinating their children for personal or philosophical reasons, and most states have religious exemptions. According to the Centers for Disease Control and Prevention (CDC), the number of children under the age of two who have not been vaccinated has quadrupled since 2001. Research has shown unvaccinated children are 23 times more likely to develop whooping cough and 35 times more likely to be infected with measles. Unvaccinated children are 6.5 times more likely to be hospitalized with pneumonia than vaccinated children. The CDC has also estimated that for children born between 1998 and 2013, vaccinations have prevented more than twenty million hospitalizations and 730,000 deaths.

Generally, some critical thinking and skepticism are important traits to have if you want to discern fact from fiction, but too much skepticism can be dangerous. Some pharmaceutical companies have done unethical or dangerous things in the name of selling medications, and money can influence science and government. Still, blanket distrust of these actors has contributed to the rise in anti-vaxxers, demonstrating how someone can use critical thinking poorly or to draw incorrect conclusions. In *Factfulness*, Rosling writes, "In a devastating example of critical thinking gone bad, highly educated, deeply caring parents avoid the vaccinations that would protect their children from killer diseases."

Before the advent of routine chicken pox inoculations for school-going children in 1995, there were about four million cases of chicken pox a year, with 100 to 150 deaths. Thanks to vaccinations, the death toll from chicken pox has dropped by 90 percent, and outbreaks are rare. When they do occur,

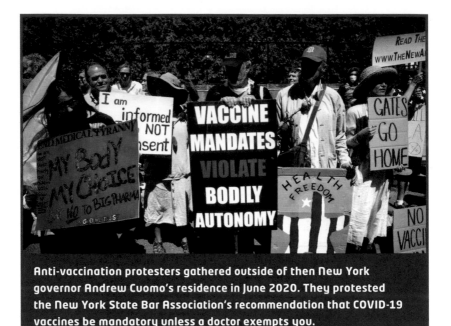

Anti-vaccination protesters gathered outside of then New York governor Andrew Cuomo's residence in June 2020. They protested the New York State Bar Association's recommendation that COVID-19 vaccines be mandatory unless a doctor exempts you.

studies show an association between outbreaks in an area and the prevalence of anti-vaxxers. In 2015 North Carolina state legislators tried to overturn a clause that allowed religious exemption to vaccinations. Their attempts were met with vociferous protests, and they were accused of "medical terrorism." The bill was withdrawn, and in November 2018 a chicken pox outbreak occurred at Asheville Waldorf School. It was the largest chicken pox outbreak in North Carolina in twenty years. Two-thirds of the students in the school were not vaccinated, one of the highest exemption rates in the state.

The CDC keeps track of all cases of measles in the United States. There were outbreaks in 2014, 2015, 2017, 2018, and 2019. All occurred in undervaccinated populations. The 2014 outbreak occurred among unvaccinated Amish communities in Ohio. The infamous Disneyland outbreak occurred in 2015, and it is estimated that about half the people that contracted the measles in that outbreak had not been vaccinated. A small outbreak in 2017 occurred among a largely unvaccinated Somali-American community in Minnesota. A measles outbreak among the orthodox Jewish community in Brooklyn and Rockland forced city officials to order mandatory immunizations for unvaccinated citizens. Larger outbreaks of measles, chicken pox, mumps, and other diseases are more likely as fewer people get vaccinated.

Jennifer Reich, professor of sociology at the University of Colorado, Denver, studies the reasons parents reject vaccines for their children. She found that they work very hard to keep current with the latest information about vaccines and want to do what is best for their children. "Many 'anti-vax' parents see themselves as experts on their own children, as best able to decide what their children need and whether their child needs a particular vaccine, and better qualified than health experts or public health agencies to decide what is best for their family. These decisions are inarguably not in the best interests of the community and indisputably increase risk to others who may be the most vulnerable to the worst outcomes of infection."

There is a lot of misinformation about the flu vaccination too. About 43 percent of Americans have the mistaken belief that one can get the flu from a vaccination, but this is not true, as the modern vaccine doesn't contain the live virus. Reich believes anti-vaxxers are no different from most other parents who don't get the flu vaccine, unnecessarily use antibiotics, or don't switch off their cars to reduce carbon dioxide emissions while waiting for their children at school pickups.

A number of studies have sought to discover how best to counter the misinformation associated with vaccines. Although these studies were done to bust flu vaccination myths, they are probably valid for all the science myths mentioned in this chapter. As with climate change skeptics, giving just the facts doesn't help. This sometimes backfires. A related approach is to try to correct an individual misconception, but for this to work, the correction has to be at least as interesting as the misinformation. Research has shown that if the truth is not as memorable, people who understood the correction and have no additional reasons, such as group identity, to oppose the correction, will nevertheless forget it within a few weeks and remember the more outrageous misconception. Unfortunately, as science writers for the Conversation say, "the best evidence suggests that a more effective way of dealing with misinformation is not spreading it in the first place." Large parts of the population may always link autism and vaccination despite any proof.

RULE 13

If you are doubtful about a medical issue, see what the FDA (Food and Drug Administration), WHO, and CDC have to say. They have the most up-to-date and accurate scientific findings, are free from outside interference, and are staffed by first-rate scientists who are charged with protecting our public health.

PLACEBOS

If your doctor gives you fake pills with detailed instructions to treat an illness, and you trust your doctor, chances are good you will feel better. This is the placebo effect. The more dramatic the fake medication seems to the patient, the larger the placebo effect. Injections are more effective than pills, and a bogus surgery is most effective of all.

Placebos won't cure you, but they can make you feel better. Purveyors of fake medicine often take advantage of the placebo effect to convince you that their products work, but clinical trials also use placebos to test the effectiveness of real treatments. In such a clinical trial, people are randomly assigned to one group that gets the real drug, while the others receive a fake drug, or placebo, that they believe is the real thing. If the researchers find no significant difference between the effects of the placebo and those of the drug being tested, then they can conclude that the drug did not work.

The best clinical trials are also double-blind—to remove any bias and preconceived ideas about the effectiveness of the drug, neither the researchers nor the research participants know who is getting active medication and who receives the placebo.

RULE 14

If a study used human subjects, check to see whether they used a placebo-controlled double-blind clinical trial. The size of the trial is also important because when more patients are enrolled, safety issues and beneficial effects are seen sooner and the differences between the patients with the real medication and those with the placebo are more obvious. Clinical trials can have thousands of subjects. When scientific studies involving humans are smaller, the researchers involved should address how they have achieved the statistical confidence they claim to have.

GENETICALLY MODIFIED ORGANISMS

Syndicated columnist Michael Gerson was appalled to find that his dog's food was prominently labeled as containing no genetically modified organisms (GMOs). "Some food companies seem to be saying that GMO ingredients are not even fit for your dog," he wrote. "These brands are guilty of crimes against rationality." His writing is a response to a recent rise in anti-GMO sentiment in public discourse.

GMOs are organisms that have been genetically altered in the laboratory so that they express new, desired traits. Livestock, food crops, and pets are often genetically modified.

Genes are made up of deoxyribonucleic acid (DNA), a chainlike molecule packed inside the nucleus of the cell. Each DNA molecule is made of a series of four base chemicals: thymine (T), adenine (A), cytosine (C), and guanine (G). The sequence, or arrangement, of the bases determines an organism's traits. One can think of DNA as a large cookbook that contains all the recipes that are required to make every kind of protein found in the body. Scientists call the recipes *genes*. Genes carry the instructions for how each living thing will grow, function, and reproduce.

Every cell has all the recipes required to make every protein that is found in the body. When a cell in your finger needs to make more muscle, the molecular machinery of that cell will find the recipes for the required proteins and make them. Unless something goes wrong, that cell will never make a protein that isn't needed in the finger. The complete set of instructions on how to make all the proteins in the body is the genome (in essence, the recipe book). Humans are made up of about ten trillion cells, each cell has a nucleus, and each nucleus has a complete set of instructions. If one could stretch the DNA from one human cell in a straight line, it would be about 6.6 feet (2 m) long. Taking the entire DNA from all the cells in one person would produce a DNA string that could stretch from Earth to the sun and back again more than fifty times.

Using biomolecular techniques, it is possible to genetically modify a living organism—plant or animal—so that it contains a gene from another organism. In genetically modified foods, the new gene bestows the organism with a new, desirable property, such as the production of more vitamins, a longer shelf life, easier harvesting, or a better taste. To create a GMO, you need to identify a particular trait you want in your organism, find the gene that is responsible for the property in another organism, insert the gene into the correct organism, and then breed the GMO. For example, say you wanted to make spicy strawberries. You could take the gene that creates the spicy chemicals found in chili peppers, give that gene to strawberries, and then grow a field of these new spiceberries.

Scientists use a number of methods to insert the genes with the desired traits into the host species. One method is to insert the DNA into a benign, or harmless, virus and use a syringe to inject the virus into an animal's bloodstream. The virus then inserts the DNA into the animal's cells. Plasmids, circular strands of DNA that can replicate by themselves, and gene guns, devices that use microscopic projectiles to insert genes, are commonly used to genetically modify plants. Using CRISPR (clustered regularly interspaced short palindromic repeats), a new, very powerful technique that is the equivalent of a genetic word processor, scientists can directly change the genes of the organism or directly add new ones.

Horticulturists and farmers have also been changing the genes of plants and animals for centuries through selective breeding techniques. They interbred different species to get new and improved crops and farm animals. This was

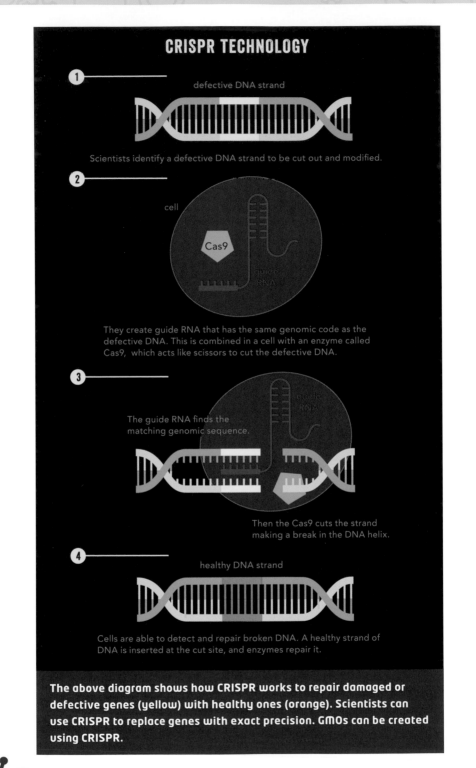

CRISPR TECHNOLOGY

1 — defective DNA strand

Scientists identify a defective DNA strand to be cut out and modified.

2 — cell

Cas9

guide RNA

They create guide RNA that has the same genomic code as the defective DNA. This is combined in a cell with an enzyme called Cas9, which acts like scissors to cut the defective DNA.

3 —

The guide RNA finds the matching genomic sequence.

guide RNA

Then the Cas9 cuts the strand making a break in the DNA helix.

4 — healthy DNA strand

Cells are able to detect and repair broken DNA. A healthy strand of DNA is inserted at the cut site, and enzymes repair it.

The above diagram shows how CRISPR works to repair damaged or defective genes (yellow) with healthy ones (orange). Scientists can use CRISPR to replace genes with exact precision. GMOs can be created using CRISPR.

fairly haphazard and not very predictable, but the process did involve humans helping to exchange genes between organisms. Lesser known is that in the last few decades, farmers have been using safe radiation and chemical methods to induce random mutations to supplement their crossbreeding attempts to achieve desirable properties such as drought tolerance, color, size, and taste. These crops are labeled as "natural" or "organic" by distributors and marketers.

Genetic engineering is a little different from selective breeding because people use biomolecular techniques to add, remove, or change genes in an organism rather than breeding. Genetic engineering thus can be much more precise and speedy. Some of the changes induced by genetic engineering could have also occurred by careful crossbreeding, but others involve taking a gene from a completely different species and adding it to the genome of a new species. Regardless, two organisms with the same genome, one created by traditional crossbreeding and the other by genetic engineering, are identical. If you think of the genome as the genetic recipe book with instructions describing how to make all the proteins in the body, then distrusting GMOs is like only using handwritten recipe books and refusing to use printed recipe books that contain the same exact text.

Many people are afraid that GMOs are allergens, toxic, or carcinogenic, or decrease the nutritional value of the food. There is no evidence of this. A 2016 National Academy of Sciences analysis of roughly one thousand studies led to the conclusion "that no differences have been found that implicate a higher risk to human health safety from these [genetically engineered] foods than from their non-GE counterparts." The American Medical Association (AMA), the American Association for the Advancement of Science, the WHO, the

THIS IS SCIENCE, NOT POLITICS

French Academy of Sciences, and the Royal Society have endorsed this view. In 2018, in contrast, 49 percent of the American public believed that foods containing genetically modified ingredients are worse for you than the equivalent foods containing no genetically modified ingredients. This number was an increase of 10 percent since 2016. About 90 percent of scientists believe GMOs are safe. Women (56 percent) are leerier of bioengineered foods than men (43 percent). However, most Americans, in contrast to Europeans, don't think about GMOs much. The increase in public distrust of genetically engineered foods has been attributed to the media creating a false balance by giving equal airtime to scientists and GMO opponents.

Besides the unfounded fear of induced toxicity or carcinogenicity, people distrust GMOs for other reasons, some less legitimate than others. Perhaps the most common reason is a philosophical one: a preference for nature and small family farms and an aversion to technology, especially products developed by big agricultural companies such as Monsanto. Nothing is wrong with having a preference for non-GMO foods for philosophical reasons, but one could not use these reasons to argue that GMOs are unsafe.

Some people worry about long-term effects of GMOs that haven't appeared in scientific studies or that GMOs will have ecological effects that have not been observed yet. Many misguided nongovernmental organizations play up these fears by using terms such as "Frankenfoods" to refer to GMOs. Many producers reinforce these fears by selling "safe" GMO-free foods.

Finally, many people have the incorrect belief that natural or organic foods are safer than foods with synthetic additives. This is wrong. First, "synthetic" and "genetically engineered"

A wheat variety called EcoWheat, developed by agricultural biotech company Bioceres in 2020, is genetically modified to be drought tolerant.

do not refer to the same processes, and second, a food that is "natural" is not necessarily less toxic. Any food in excessive quantities will harm your body—even too much water can be toxic. Consumers should have the right to know when foods have been modified. They should also learn about genetic modifications and weigh the pros and cons of specific products. By understanding how genetic engineering works and the compositions of all our foods, we are empowered to make intelligent, science-based decisions about what we eat.

There is a wide range of possible genetic modifications. Some are trivial, some are dangerous, and some can save millions of lives. One lifesaving genetic modification involves photosynthesis in plants. Evolution isn't perfect, and most crops have an imperfect photosynthetic system. They lose many calories of energy to a wasteful process called photorespiration that doesn't do anything useful. In 2019 Donald Ort, the Robert Emerson Professor of Plant Biology and Crop Sciences at the University of Illinois, published a paper in *Science* in which he and his collaborators described a genetically modified tobacco plant that has a much more efficient photosynthetic system. The GMO tobacco plants grew faster, taller, and produced 40 percent more biomass. Tobacco was used in the studies because it is an ideal model organism for other crops, such as soybeans, cowpeas, rice, potatoes, tomatoes, and eggplants, so the researchers believed the modification could work in these crops. If it does, it is a game changer. According to Ort, "We could feed up to 200 million additional people with the calories lost to photorespiration in the Midwestern US each year."

TRUSTING SCIENCE

A significant portion of the general public distrusts scientific evidence about the safety of genetically modified foods, whether vaccinations cause autism, and whether human activities are responsible for climate change. These people have bought into a false picture of science. They believe that there is only 100 percent consensus or no consensus. As scientists make new findings, we publish them in peer-reviewed journals. The more such pieces we have, the more of the puzzle we can see. If 90 percent of the puzzle is complete, we have a good idea of what it is showing us. There is still a huge danger in overinterpreting individual puzzle pieces and in trying to place false pieces (fake news and predatory journals) into a puzzle. But just because we haven't completed the whole puzzle doesn't mean we don't know what is going on.

Many areas of science have been politicized, and our cognitive biases influence us to not believe real news.

This problem is exacerbated because most people get their news exclusively from sources whose political bias they agree with. Some news sources will present two sides of an issue as if they are equally supported by science. Then skeptics believe that their view is more common than it is.

Hans Rosling would like to ask all skeptics, "What kind of evidence would convince you to change your mind?" If the answer is, "No evidence could ever change my mind," that shows that the deniers have placed themselves outside of evidence-based rationality and critical thinking. Rosling says for the deniers, to be consistent in their skepticism about science, "next time you have an operation, please ask your surgeon not to bother washing her hands."

In one of his opinion pieces, Michael Gerson writes, "Our deepest beliefs should help navigate reality, not determine it." He is right. In the long run, disregarding science and scientific experts will serve no political cause well.

RULE 15

Ask yourself what evidence would convince you to change your mind. If there is no evidence, then beware of your own critical thinking.

4

QUACKERY

Quacks, humbugs, charlatans, and swindlers take advantage of people's inability to differentiate between fact and fiction and on fears of sickness and death. They do this by selling untested, unsafe, and very expensive fake medicines, health supplements, and stem cell treatments. Sometimes they truly believe that what they are selling works. In the past, quacks and charlatans occasionally pushed the envelope of conventionality and challenged the status quo. But you must be very careful before entrusting your health to quacks of the type described in this chapter.

One famous quack was Robert Talbor (1642–1681). Although he lived more than three hundred years ago, he was a prototypical medical charlatan, or scammer, whose techniques continue to inspire quacks in the twenty-first century. In particular, he took advantage of one of the biggest breakthroughs in the fight against malaria. In 1640 Jesuit theologian Juan de Lugo reported that a tincture of cinchona bark was commonly used to treat malaria in South America. By 1656 the British were drinking an infusion of the cinchona bark to avoid the disease. However, British people were less likely to use the treatment than the Spanish or Italians. In England, cinchona bark was known as the "Jesuits' bark," and there was some resistance to drinking the hot and bitter remedy due to its strong association with Catholicism. Talbor manipulated the situation to make his fortune. He was a self-educated doctor who saw the effectiveness of the unpopular cinchona bark brew in treating malaria fevers. Talbor concocted a cinchona, wine, and opium mixture that was still effective but lacked the bitter taste of the original medicine—and had some other interesting side effects. Deceiving his customers about the product, he sold this secret fever remedy as a safe alternative to the cinchona bark as a cure untainted by Catholicism.

Word of his success at treating malarial fevers spread rapidly. In 1672 King Charles II appointed him royal physician, and Talbor was knighted in 1678. He became the physician of choice to royalty all over Europe. King Louis XIV of France paid Talbor three thousand gold crowns and gave him a large pension and a title, and in return, Talbor promised to reveal his secret formula upon his death. Despite serving the royals of Europe, Talbor was not satisfied with his fame and fortune. He clandestinely bought up all the cinchona bark to prevent any competition.

Talbor's manipulations of the early pharmaceutical market did not last long. In 1681 he died at the age of thirty-nine.

As promised, his secret was revealed to King Louis XIV, and in 1682 an English translation was published of *The English Remedy, or, Talbor's Wonderful Secret for the Cureing of Agues and Feavers Sold by the Author, Sir Robert Talbor to the Most Christian King and since His Death Ordered by His Majesty to Be Published in French, for the Benefit of His Subjects; and Now Translated into English for Publick Good*. Talbor's secret remedy was secret no more.

Talbor used an existing medicine and put his own spin on it. He was a good salesman and a shrewd businessman who made and used his connections with celebrities. These are characteristics of quacks through the ages.

In the late nineteenth and early twentieth centuries, newspapers were crammed with quacks hawking their wares, such as Mrs. Winslow's Soothing Syrup, which was sold as a cure-all medicine for fussy babies and contained high concentrations of alcohol and some morphine. These substances are obviously dangerous for infants, and the US government has since outlawed or regulated their use in common medicines. Modern medical scammers no longer add opium and morphine to their products, but some still use untested substances.

By the 1920s, the AMA had managed to prevent purveyors of unproven medicines from publishing in medical journals and from advertising in newspapers. But the good work the association had done was negated by the advent of radio. By the 1930s, 40 percent of Americans had a radio, and that number rose to 83 percent by the 1940s. The quacks took advantage of the new uncontrolled media space and hit the airwaves in a big way. In 1932 the Federal Radio Commission tried to banish fortune-tellers, mystics, seers, and other people peddling dubious claims from the airwaves. The quacks simply moved south of the US–Mexico border and continued broadcasting, and "the AMA lamented that no adequate and prompt measures are as yet available to curb venal radio stations from selling 'time' to anyone who pays the price."

One such radio show host and quack to have his radio license revoked by the Federal Radio Commission was John R. Brinkley (1885–1942). The eloquent Brinkley used his radio show to convince men to pay good money for goat gonads to be grafted into their testicles. This was supposed to make them as virile as goats, according to Brinkley. The AMA investigated Brinkley, finding that although he wasn't a certified doctor, he really did what he promised. The only hitch was that having goat gonads in their testicles didn't actually improve men's sex lives or increase their virility.

Shirley W. Wynne (1882–1942), then the New York City commissioner of health, had some advice for radio listeners. The human body is complex, and for many diseases, real doctors can't promise and would never advertise that they can cure a disease. Beware of things that sound too good to be true.

RULE 16

To sell their medical products and procedures, medical scammers often use testimonials of patients. Beware of medical products that sound unbelievably good and that claim to cure many different diseases. Testimonials are not a substitute for scientific proof, and real doctors would never promise results, because health is impossible to guarantee.

Wynne's advice is still valid in a world dominated by the largely unregulated internet. Advertisements for unverified medical treatments take advantage of various techniques, including emotional testimonials from patients, to convince you of their effectiveness. One must think critically and be skeptical of these testimonials and any medication that claims to be an indiscriminate cure-all. Be sure to do a lot of research on procedures, tests, medications, or supplements that your doctor hasn't prescribed you so that you don't waste your money buying fake medicine.

SUPPLEMENTS

Prevagen, a dietary supplement that purports to combat memory loss due to aging, is a typical example of a supplement that is dressed to look like medication. Ads for Prevagen appeared on TV at the same time that the supplement's manufacturer, Quincy Bioscience, was involved in numerous judicial trials alleging that the company falsely advertised the cognitive benefits of Prevagen.

Prevagen claims to be a dietary supplement that "has been clinically shown to help with mild memory loss associated with aging." The supposed active ingredient, apoaequorin, is derived from jellyfish. In the US, the product had sales of $165 million between 2007 and mid-2015, and its ads became a common sight on Fox News, CNN, and NBC, during the evening news, on *Jeopardy*, and during popular sports events such as NFL games. The ad claims, "Your brain is an amazing thing. But as you get older, it naturally begins to change, causing a lack of sharpness or even trouble with recall. Thankfully, the breakthrough in Prevagen helps your brain and actually improves memory. The secret is an ingredient originally discovered in jellyfish. In clinical trials, Prevagen has been shown to improve short term memory."

This ad clearly promises something unbelievable: the improvement of short-term memory. Viewers should be skeptical, especially when they see in small writing at the bottom of the screen, "These statements have not been evaluated by the FDA. This product is not intended to treat, cure, or prevent any disease." This and that the clinical trial referred to in the advertisement was an unpublished study of 218 human subjects doing nine different computer-assessed cognitive tasks indicate that the supplement is probably a scam.

The ad ends with an image of the Prevagen box, the pill bottle, and the logos of Walgreens, CVS, and Rite Aid, leaving the viewer with the impression that the product is endorsed by these pharmacies. Many local pharmacies do stock Prevagen, selling bottles of thirty pills for about forty dollars. At this cost, the pills, which are not covered by any health insurance, may appeal to the desperate. Julie Nepveu, a senior attorney for the AARP Foundation, says, "Supplement companies have keyed into the idea that older people are going to spend a ton of money on their products because they want to feel better." Quincy has made tens of millions of dollars selling Prevagen at thirty-three to sixty dollars for a month's supply.

Prevagen is a dietary supplement and not a drug. That's why it's not regulated by the FDA. As a dietary supplement, it is legally classed as a food and, instead, falls under the jurisdiction of the Federal Trade Commission (FTC). But the FTC has been repeatedly rebuffed in its efforts to regulate supplements like the FDA regulates drugs. For example, in a crucial precedent-setting case on April 18, 2017, Judge John Michael Vazquez ruled in favor of pharmaceutical company Bayer in a lawsuit over its probiotic dietary supplement, Phillips' Colon Health. The consumers who filed the lawsuit argued

Prevagen is among many supplements that supposedly improve memory. Be wary of supplements and the claims they make regarding your health.

that no clinical tests or peer-reviewed papers supported the company's claims that its supplement could help with various dietary ailments. But Vazquez held that showing that the claims are unsubstantiated is insufficient—one has to prove that the statements are actually false. In other words, the mere absence of scientific evidence wasn't enough to charge Bayer with making false claims. Because of this ruling, supplement manufacturers can make claims about the efficacy of their products without having to do clinical tests or submitting their results to peer review. And if the FTC wants to contest those claims, it has to provide the clinical trials that prove that the statements are false.

RULE 17

If a supplement tries to look like a medicine, beware.

In an era when the importance of facts and truths has been devalued, it is not surprising that Prevagen and its compatriots are able to continue advertising and selling fake goods.

STEM CELLS

Stem cell clinics are popping up all over the United States. They have grown from just two in 2009 to more than seven hundred by 2017. From 2014 to 2016, at least one hundred new clinics opened in the US. These clinics are following on the heels of those that were established in countries including China, South Korea, and Mexico where they targeted Americans as "medical tourists." Thousands of Americans travel abroad to seek medical care each year, often because desired treatments are cheaper abroad or only available in other countries. A 2019 study of medical marketing in the US showed that stem cell clinics have boosted their marketing from $900,000 in 2012 to $11.3 million in 2016.

The two most important properties of stem cells are their ability to undergo self-renewal and to change into new cell types. They can multiply to form many daughter cells. These can then differentiate, or change into new cell types, as required. Stem cells derived from embryos are called embryonic stem cells and are tremendously good at replicating. They can be differentiated into any type of adult cell. Stem cells obtained from adults are less good at dividing and can only differentiate into a limited number of cell types.

In regenerative medicine, scientists guide stem cells in the process of differentiation to replace damaged or diseased tissue. Stem cell research has matured enough that the first carefully regulated human trials have begun. Researchers are already working on stem cell therapies for spinal cord injuries, type 1 diabetes, Parkinson's disease, amyotrophic lateral

STEM CELL DIFFERENTIATION

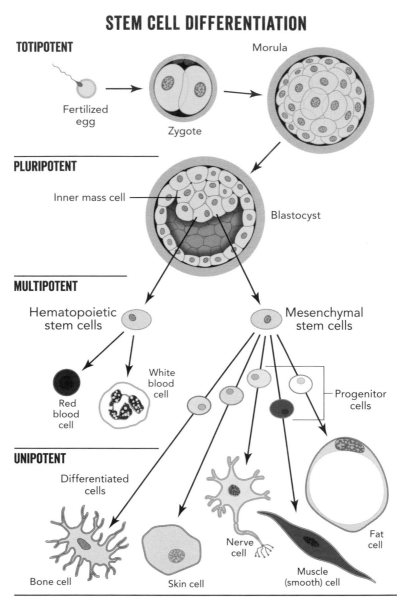

Source: Mairead Hayes, Gerard Curley, Bilal Ansari, and John G. Laffey, "Clinical Review: Stem Cell Therapies for Acute Lung Injury/Acute Respiratory Distress Syndrome - Hope or Hype?," *Critical Care* 16, no. 205 (2012), https://ccforum.biomedcentral.com/articles/10.1186/cc10570.

Stem cells are the body's raw materials—cells from which all other cells with specialized functions are generated. Pluripotent stem cells can develop into any cell type or tissue the body needs. Embryonic stem cells are pluripotent. Multipotent stem cells can develop into multiple kinds of cells and are more limited than pluripotent stem cells. Unipotent stem cells can only develop into one specific cell type, such as muscle cells.

sclerosis, Alzheimer's disease, heart disease, stroke, burns, cancer, and osteoarthritis. The problem is that unscrupulous stem cell clinics are undermining the field by skipping ahead without doing efficacy or safety studies. Instead, they are selling spots in their so-called medical trials.

The FDA has issued the following warning, "Stem cell products have the potential to treat many medical conditions and diseases. But for almost all of these products, it is not yet known whether the product has any benefit—or if the product is safe to use." The only FDA-approved stem-cell–based products are blood-forming stem cells derived from umbilical cords. Stem cell therapies have numerous dangers. The stem cells could differentiate into the wrong cell types or into the right cell types but be nonfunctioning. They can grow irregularly, induce an immune response, or cause a tumor growth. Consumers should only consider FDA-approved treatments or studies being done under an investigational new drug application, which is a clinical investigation plan submitted and allowed to proceed by the FDA. Patients should also not have to pay to be part of a medical trial.

Age-related macular degeneration mainly affects people over fifty years old. It is the most common ocular disease in the developed world, causing more than 50 percent of all cases of visual impairment. The disease affects cells in the macula, which is in the center of the retina in the back of the eye. In a small clinical trial that sought to determine if stem cell therapies could treat age-related macular degeneration, researchers from the University of California, Santa Barbara, turned stem cells into retinal pigment epithelium cells (a single layer of cells outside the retina that have several important functions associated with vision). They then collaborated with surgeons from Moorfields Eye Hospital, London, to use a specially engineered surgical tool to insert the patch of epithelial cells under the retinas of two patients. The operation lasted one to two hours and was a great success. An eighty-six-year-old man and a woman in her early sixties went from not being able to read at all, even with glasses, to being able to read sixty to eighty words a minute with normal reading glasses. "This study represents real progress in regenerative medicine and opens the door on new treatment options for people with age-related macular degeneration," said University of California, Santa Barbara, coauthor Peter Coffey.

Doing research of this nature is a slow methodical process, regulated by the FDA and its international counterparts. Small numbers of patients are treated at first, only one eye is done, and there is a comparison group (patients who do not receive the trial treatment) and a long follow-up. This paper was only written after the two subjects had been observed for twelve months after the operation. It will take years before this treatment has been rigorously tested and has been safely taken to the market.

But stem cell clinics are unregulated. They use false results or take advantage of results such as those described in the paragraph above to attract patients for stem cell replacement surgeries, circumventing the FDA approval process. They use high-pressure sales techniques to recruit their patients, which include on-the-spot discounts, emotional patient-testimonial videos, and slick recruitment videos. Surgeries range from $2,000 to $20,000. Patients who can't afford the fees are advised to start GoFundMe pages and to get the money from family and friends. A study on stem cell clinics published in June 2019 revealed that more than half the clinics employed no physicians trained to deal with the medical conditions advertised.

Stem Cell Center of Georgia is in the Ageless Wellness Center in suburban Atlanta. It was founded in 2008, specializing in Botox treatment, laser hair removal, and other beauty treatments. In 2014 the center added stem cell treatments to its menu. One patient, Doris Tyler, was losing her sight due to age-related macular degeneration. In 2016 she signed up for the stem cell treatment at the Stem Cell Center of Georgia. The clinic claimed they could take stem cells from her fat and inject them into her eyes, where they would halt or even cure the macular degeneration. Hers was the first time the clinic tried this procedure.

Five days after the operation, the Stem Cell Center of Georgia boasted of its success on its Facebook page and urged customers to book appointments. But Tyler's vision was becoming blurry, her retina detached, and despite numerous corrective surgeries, she totally lost her vision in a few months. Tyler and her husband sued the clinic. Three other women have lost their sight in similar procedures done in a Florida clinic, the US Stem Cell Clinic. The clinic has since settled the three cases and has stopped doing eye injections. Despite this, the clinic has expanded by opening a new clinic in a central Florida senior living community and has added stem cell treatments of erectile dysfunction to its procedures.

The stem cell clinics are not regulated by the FDA, as they obtain their stem cells from the patients themselves and therefore the stem cells can't be considered as new drugs. But the FDA has promised to crack down on stem cell clinics, particularly those that are performing dangerous operations such as injections into the eyes, spinal cord, or brain. The clinics and their doctors cite testimonials of "cured" patients as evidence that their treatments work and say that customers should be allowed to sign up for experimental treatments, claiming it is their right to make such decisions for their own health. Timothy Caulfield, a health law professor at the

University of Alberta, disagrees. He says, "What they're really selling is false hope. It's science-ploitation. They're taking a legitimate and developing field of science and using it to prey on patients who are desperate for a cure."

Charles Murry, director of the Institute for Stem Cell and Regenerative Medicine at the University of Washington, is "afraid that these charlatans will besmirch the reputation of legitimate work we have spent decades trying to bring to [clinics]."

Scientists are always finding new promising leads that could open the door to a revolution in medicine. Mostly, they end up being dead ends, such as treatments that don't translate from mouse studies to human patients, or those that have undesirable or dangerous side effects. None of this bothers quacks. They have found ways of hitching their schemes to legitimate research breakthroughs as they make their path from promise to discarded dream.

RULE 18

Beware of clinics that use high-pressure sales techniques to recruit their patients, which include on-the-spot discounts, emotional patient-testimonial videos, and slick recruitment videos.

PARABIOSIS

In 1864 Paul Bert removed the skin from the sides of two albino rats and stitched the two rats together so that they had a shared circulatory system, as found in conjoined twins and between a mother and her unborn child. He injected fluid into one rat and showed how the fluid flowed into the other. This was the first reported joining of the vascular system of two separate living organisms, and so parabiosis (from Greek, "para" meaning *between*, and "bios" meaning *lives*) was invented.

The technique underwent a significant resurgence when Clive McCay, a professor of animal husbandry at Cornell University, discovered that young blood rejuvenates old tissues. In 1956 his students joined sixty-nine pairs of rats, each pair containing one young and one old rat. It wasn't a great success, as eleven pairs died from a mysterious condition the researchers called parabiotic disease, and they found that "if two rats are not adjusted to each other, one will chew the head of the other until it is destroyed." Later studies by the same group showed that a shared circulation increased the bone density of older rats. In the 1970s, other groups showed that in some cases shared vascular systems could lead to prolonged life for the older partner, but the field fell out of favor as institutional approval for animal studies became more demanding. That all changed in the past few years as potentially promising results came out of new studies that used mice. The researchers socialized the mice prior to parabiosis to ensure the animals would get along, and only joined mice of the same sex and size. By connecting the circulatory system of young mice with those of old mice, researchers made the old mice healthier, smarter, and stronger, and even gave them shinier fur.

Initial studies from Amy Wagers's laboratory at the Harvard Department of Stem Cell and Regenerative Biology have shown that the growth differentiation factor 11, a protein found in young blood, may be responsible for the increase in strength and stamina observed in old mice after parabiosis. "We're not de-ageing animals," says Wagers, "We're restoring function to tissues."

In 2014 Tony Wyss-Coray, a neurologist at Stanford University, and his collaborators published a paper in *Nature Medicine*, a specialized magazine run by *Nature*, in which they described that young blood plasma stimulated neuronal growth in old mice. "We didn't have to exchange the whole blood," said Wyss-Coray. "It acts like a drug." Based on their results, they formed a biotech company, Alkahest. It is conducting randomized, placebo-controlled, double-blind clinical trials on the effect of parabiosis on Alzheimer's and Parkinson's disease. The company is not interested in opening a clinic. The aim is to develop drugs for age-related diseases. When "there's just no clinical evidence [that the treatment will be beneficial] . . . you're basically abusing people's trust and the public excitement around this," says Wyss-Coray.

Of course, that hasn't stopped quacks and charlatans, even if all they have going for them is a strong placebo effect. Pointing to this research, some clinics perform blood transfusions between young people and older patients. The combined drama of getting blood from a strapping young person and the promising mouse experimental data are often enough to make patients feel younger.

In 2019 *Men's Health* (not a peer-reviewed journal) had a piece, "People Are Getting Transfusions with Young People's Blood to Fight Aging." The article discusses the work of Ambrosia, a company that, for about $8,000, will infuse you with about 2 quarts (2 L) of plasma taken from some sixteen- to twenty-five-year-old donors. The procedure takes one to two days. Jesse Karmazin, founder of the company, says they have done about 150 transfusions, and many of his patients report feeling better and have improved memory, sleep, and appearance with just one treatment a year. Karmazin claims he has done a preliminary study of eighty-one patients who paid for their own treatments. Allegedly, the 2017 study showed improvement in markers for Alzheimer's, heart disease, and inflammation, but by 2021 it had not been published. According to Ambrosia's website, patients can have blood shipped to a nearby physician, and the company accepts payment via PayPal. Because these clinics are essentially doing blood transfusions, the procedures are automatically approved by the FDA, and Ambrosia doesn't have to prove that its treatment has any benefits.

Dr. Dipnarine Maharaj, a Scottish-trained hematologist and oncologist, has upped the ante. He is selling spots in his clinical trials for $285,000. For this price, patients get monthly infusions of plasma obtained from young donors who were injected with a drug designed to stimulate bone marrow to make more white blood cells and stem cells. In an article for Stat magazine, science journalist Rebecca Robbins asked eight independent

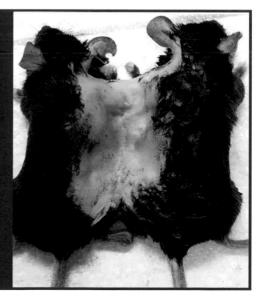

Parabiosis is the connection of two animals so that they share their blood circulation. While parabiosis has shown promising results in mice and rats, this doesn't necessarily translate to human beings, and parabiosis is not the same procedure as the blood transfusions that some quacks try to sell to people.

experts to review Maharaj's informational handouts about the clinical trial. They all sharply criticized the studies' scientific rationale. Michael Conboy, a cell and molecular biologist at the University of California, Berkeley, who has done parabiosis studies, said that "it just reeks of [quackery]. There's no evidence in my mind that it's going to work." When Robbins asked Maharaj for the scientific basis of his expensive clinical trials, Maharaj provided her with six papers that were fundamental to his work. Amy Wagers, who is a coauthor on three of the papers, said in an email to Stat that she does not agree that her teams' studies provide any scientific basis for Maharaj's clinical trial.

DR. OZ

Kelly McBride, vice president of the Poynter Institute, a nonprofit journalism school in St. Petersburg, Florida, thinks that fake medical news is worse than and more common than any other type of fake news. A lot of it comes from quacks and charlatans who want to make a quick buck, as evidenced in the stem cell and parabiosis examples. But a substantial amount of fake news is generated by journalists and TV hosts. According to McBride, these reporters struggle with the fact that "journalism is very much about trying to simplify and distribute information about what's new and where advances have been made. That's incompatible with the scientific process, which can take a long time to build a body of evidence," and that "good information can be really boring."

The Dr. Oz Show has an estimated daily audience of four million viewers. Dr. Mehmet Oz got his start on The Oprah Winfrey Show, where he was so popular that he got his own show in 2009. Both Time and Esquire magazines have had him on their "most influential people" lists. To keep up such a high profile and enthrall viewers, Oz had to make wild claims and present exciting medical advice. A 2014 study published in the *British Medical Journal* examined the recommendations made in forty randomly chosen episodes of *The Dr. Oz Show* from 2013. They found that 15 percent of his recommendations were completely contradicted by peer-reviewed medical journals and there was no evidence for 39 percent of his assertions. The *British Medical Journal* paper is not the first peer-reviewed article to call out Oz by name. In 2013 the journal *Nutrition and Cancer* published "Reality Check: There Is No Such Thing as a Miracle Food." The paper was written to warn doctors and patients that statements Oz made about "miracle foods" that could decrease the risk of ovarian cancer had no medical evidence to back them up. Oz has also been castigated by the Senate Subcommittee on Consumer Protection, Product Safety, and Data Security and by the FTC for using his show to deceive audiences and sell products, particularly diet supplements—belly blasters and mega metabolism boosters. He very rarely discloses any conflicts of interests or commercial interests he has with products he endorses on his show.

In response to criticisms, Oz has invoked his right to free speech, a conspiracy by the pro-GMO lobby to undermine him, and said that "I want folks to realize that I'm a doctor, and I'm coming into their lives to be supportive of them. But it's not a medical show." In the show, however, he is called "Dr. Oz," wears medical scrubs, and dispenses medical advice. After all the complaints, petitions, and subpoenas, Oz still hosts anti-vaxxers on his show and pushes miracle elixirs (cure-alls), homeopathy, imaginary energies, and psychics who communicate with the dead. He regularly uses words like "miracle" and "magic." In 2018 he filmed the episode

Oz is an enormously popular celebrity with a huge audience. In 2014 he was questioned by Congress's Subcommittee on Consumer Protection for his promotion of questionable weight loss supplements. Congressional members pointed out that he could instead use his show to promote scientifically sound medical advice, and Oz responded that he believes in the products he promotes.

"Your Personal Health Horoscope" in which he interviewed an astrologer about what one's astrological sign can tell someone about their health. Despite all the bad publicity and the obvious quackery, Oz's audience grows. He won a daytime Emmy Award in 2018, and his show was released in China in 2019. In May 2018 then president Donald Trump appointed Oz to the President's Council on Sports, Fitness & Nutrition. He has written ten books and has his own magazine.

Despite Oz's claims that he is merely an entertainer, many people in his audience do take his medical advice seriously. On March 17, 2020, French investigators posted a preprint clinical paper online touting the successful use of hydroxychloroquine, an anti-malaria drug, in treating COVID-19 patients. The paper was very preliminary and deeply flawed. Nevertheless, Oz enthusiastically promoted the work. His misguided advocacy of the anti-malaria drugs hydroxychloroquine and chloroquine led Trump to promote its use too and to take hydroxychloroquine as a preventive measure.

In response to presidential pressure, the FDA used its emergency authority to permit the use of hydroxychloroquine in a way for which it wasn't tested or approved. This has resulted in drug shortages for people who take hydroxychloroquine to treat autoimmune diseases, reduced enrollment in clinical trials of other potential treatments, and reports of illness and death linked to chloroquinine overdoses in the US and Nigeria.

The WHO has recommended that the anti-malarial drugs only be taken for COVID-19 if it is part of a clinical trial. And the United States' National Institutes of Health reported that there was insufficient data to recommend either for or against the use of hydroxychloroquine and chloroquinine. "Doctors are just trying it because they want to offer their patients something," says Lauren Sauer, an emergency medicine researcher at Johns Hopkins University. "Anecdotes have turned

RULE 19

TV hosts and journalists generate a substantial amount of fake news. To get our attention, morning shows and talk shows need something exciting and new, and not necessarily correct, to report on. Entertainers such as Oz, Dr. Phil (McGraw), and Dr. Drew (Pinsky) should not be your go-to medical sources.

into evidence, it seems." For some time after the FDA invoked its emergency authority, there were more than one hundred hydroxychloroquine and chloroquinine clinical trials enrolling more than one hundred thousand patients. But none of the trials presented positive results, and most of the remaining trials were canceled—but not before they diverted important resources and attention from other potential treatments.

WELLNESS

Oz is a big proponent of "wellness." Wellness is a hard concept to define, but many consider it an all-encompassing state of well-being, a positive presence rather than the simple absence of disease. Wellness isn't necessarily medicine, but it fills some gaps left by the medical industry. Its popularity may be a reaction to our often hectic and stressful modern lives, and even a reaction against the commercialization of medicine. In 2017 the wellness industry made more than $4.2 trillion. The personal care, beauty, and antiaging segment of the industry made $1.08 trillion by itself, more than the pharmaceutical industry.

Women are the primary target of wellness marketeers. Doctors sometimes don't take the time to listen to patients, particularly women, when they talk about their health issues. For example, researchers from the University of Florida and the Mayo Clinic monitored conversations between doctors and patients and found that patients were given an average of eleven seconds to explain why they were seeking treatment before they were interrupted. Caulfield, the professor at the University of Alberta, says, "Even if the clinical advice is sound, the idea of not being listened to matters. And there is evidence that women's issues aren't taken as seriously. Their problems aren't being heard. That matters. Those are real problems."

To understand why people are attracted to wellness scams, Caulfield visited many wellness practitioners. He reports that "I've gone to a lot of different alternative practitioners: reflexologists, acupuncturists, reiki, cupping. Almost without exception, it's been a positive experience. Someone is listening to your problems. With traditional healthcare, it's always a pretty miserable experience."

Genuine wellness practitioners and wellness quacks fill the void created by a stressed medical care system. Science, especially medical science, historically has neglected women, and some take advantage of this. When it comes to women's health, Amy Miller, president and CEO of the Society for Women's Health Research, says, "there's a lot we don't know. We only started including women in research [fifteen] or [twenty] years ago and that means a lot of generic drugs may not have been investigated in women. We don't know if a drug isn't as effective in a woman's body as it is in a man's. And then there are areas where there is nothing on the market [for women]." It wasn't until 2016 that the National Institutes of Health required all the researchers it funded to use both male and female mice in their studies and to use male and female tissue cells in their research. Perhaps it is understandable then that people, especially women, are looking elsewhere for their medical solutions and are vulnerable to pseudoscience.

A 2019 article in *Marie Claire*, "The Wellness Industry Isn't Making You Well," sums up some of the problems with the industry: it labels certain bodies as good and others as bad and it promotes products and services that are prohibitively expensive for many.

The industry also distorts science to make a profit, potentially damaging both science as well as the patient. Wellness appears in this book because, "in its current form, wellness isn't filling in the gaps left by medicine. It's exploiting them."

Activated charcoal is a good example of how the wellness industry uses legitimate science to make lots of money in a manner similar to that seen in stem cell and parabiosis clinics. Chemists use activated charcoal as a filter to remove contaminants and impurities from solutions. Activated carbon has an extensive surface area, which can take in pollutants through adsorption, a process where a thin layer of material adheres to the surface of another substance. Emergency room doctors use activated carbon to treat patients that have been poisoned. As the activated carbon passes through the gut, it binds all the nonpolar materials (materials that don't like water) in the gastrointestinal tract, good and bad, which are expelled in dark stool. That is good if you have just swallowed some poison by accident. It will not cure hangovers, detoxify you, reduce bloating, prevent aging, or improve your cholesterol, no matter what you hear on *The Dr. Oz Show* or read on health blogs.

One blog by famous wellness guru Dave Asprey says, "Travel, environmental pollution, and low-quality food can all put toxins in your system—and activated charcoal is the perfect solution when that toxic load gets too heavy to bear. From binding poisons to eliminating body odor, activated charcoal is loaded with benefits that can help keep toxin-induced fog and fatigue at bay." This blog entry takes a fact, that activated charcoal will indiscriminately bind all nonpolar molecules in the gastrointestinal tract (including antioxidants, medicines, and vitamins), and tries to convince the reader that charcoal can affect other systems in the body. But activated charcoal consumed by drinking cannot cross over into the circulatory system, binding to toxins in a patient's blood. Yet due to a

One popular health trend is the use of charcoal toothpaste to clean and whiten teeth. But dental health experts say that charcoal toothpaste is too abrasive for everyday use and may not get rid of stains, and any long-term effects are unknown. Despite this, some toothpaste manufacturers, such as Colgate, advertise it as a safe and effective tooth whitening and cleaning product.

psychological phenomenon called the illusory truth effect, this knowledge about charcoal doesn't necessarily protect the reader from thinking that Asprey might have a point. Even a single exposure to information that sounds as if it *could* be true—and there is often enough science in these scams to sound slightly real—can increase the perception of accuracy and tempt patients to purchase clinically unproven wellness products, such as charcoal smoothies.

QUACKS SELL PSEUDOSCIENCE

The complexity of science, the broad reach of social media, and the abundance of misinformation have made it easy for unscrupulous quacks to sell pseudoscience. Besides bilking money from their victims, quacks ferment scientific uncertainty and undermine the public trust in science and scientists. Their call for people to sign up for new, unproven techniques or to try "something natural" can lead people with serious illnesses to postpone seeking effective medical care. Both the FDA and

RULE 20

Be wary of promotions using words such as "scientific breakthrough," "miraculous cure," "secret ingredient," and "ancient remedy" and claims that the product is "natural" or "nontoxic" (which doesn't necessarily mean safe). Remember that not all chemicals are bad and that not everything natural is good.

FTC websites have pages with regularly updated health fraud news. I have converted some of the FDA warnings into rules.

Quacks often appeal to American notions of freedom and individuality, a resentment of wealthy doctors, and a desire to stay up to date with the newest trends. Quacks make unscientific claims and require society to disprove them, while doctors use proven methods in their treatments. Prosecuting even the most flagrant quackery is very difficult. To prevent it, we need to promote scientific knowledge and critical thinking, and curtail fake news.

CHAPTER 5

THE TWENTY RULES

Science is never inherently bad or evil. However, it is easy to do sloppy science, misrepresent science, or misuse science. As science grows and uncovers more knowledge, these abuses escalate proportionally. This leads to a mistrust of science instead of a culture of scientists and nonscientists finding consensus on sensitive issues. This mistrust of science is often selective: most science deniers still consult doctors when they are sick, trust that planes won't fall out of the sky, and believe that elevators will stop at the desired floor. To change the minds of deniers who don't trust scientists, researchers need to learn how to communicate with nonscientists and to talk about science

March for Science is one of many organizations advocating for science in the face of denial, fearmongering, and false balance. Learn more about March for Science at https://marchforscience.org, and be sure to check out other local and national organizations that promote science and use science-based solutions for crucial problems.

more. Scientists could develop an artificial intelligence app that gives an instant, reliable truthfulness rating to television interviews and Facebook and Twitter posts. Journalists must also refrain from using the "false balance" approach to stories about scientific findings, in which equal time is given to those with fringe views as to legitimate scientists.

The increased access to scientific knowledge has many advantages, but it has numerous disadvantages too. Scientists are losing some of their authority to the internet. This wouldn't be a problem if all the science on the web were verified, but the prevalence of fake news shows us otherwise. And peer-reviewed research is often hidden behind paywalls—it is expensive and not available to the casual searcher. The easily found material and clearly explained articles are rarely written by scientists. Sometimes journalists and TV show editors can't tell bad science from good science, and errors make their way into reporting. Quacks and charlatans take advantage of the complexity of science and the long, arduous process scientific ideas have to undergo to reach mature consensus, offering instead quick fixes or distorting research to suit their agendas.

If disbelief in science had no effect on anything but yourself, this book would not exist. But science deniers sow seeds of doubt in other people, preventing governments from acting on important issues such as climate change, damaging other people's health, and even resulting in people's deaths. That is why we need rules to distinguish real science from fake science. These twenty rules will help you to distinguish between good science and bad science, medicine and quackery, and fact and fiction.

- **RULE 1:** Research published in peer-reviewed journals has undergone rigorous quality control by experts in the field. The most important papers are published in the top peer-reviewed journals: *Science, Nature, Cell, Proceedings of the National Academy of Sciences, Journal of New England Medicine,* and the *Lancet.* If something originates from a peer-reviewed journal, it generally is legitimate.

- **RULE 2:** Research published in known predatory journals should be treated with distrust. A list of nearly twenty-five hundred known predatory journals is given at https://beallslist.net/.

- **RULE 3:** The work on preprint servers has not yet undergone peer review. If you see something that originated from a preprint server, realize that other scientists and journal editors haven't certified it as real, legitimate science yet. Rather, the authors posted it for fellow scientists to evaluate and use as building blocks for their own research. Check how long the work has been on the preprint server. If it has been more than a year and hasn't yet been published in a peer-reviewed journal, be very skeptical of it.

- **RULE 4:** Check that the research was actually done on humans. Just because a certain drug works on rats or mice does not mean it will work in humans.

- **RULE 5:** Correlation does not imply causation. Just because you can see a connection or a mutual relationship between two variables, it doesn't necessarily mean that one causes the other. Other variables might be involved.

- **RULE 6:** Beware of spectacular extraordinary claims. If you find something that makes you gasp and say, "I can't believe that," you probably shouldn't believe it without seeing really reliable proof, such as a peer-reviewed paper. Beware if a piece of news or a social media post stirs up intense feelings, especially outrage. It was most likely designed to short-circuit your critical-thinking skills by playing on your emotions.

- **RULE 7:** News that is riddled with spelling and grammatical errors is suspect. If the author couldn't be bothered to spell-check it, it likely wasn't fact-checked either.

- **RULE 8:** Although a political debate requires two opposing sides, a scientific consensus does not. Beware of "false balance," in which the media give equal time to both a scientific consensus and the fringe science or opinions that disagree with the consensus. Beware of people expressing rogue views that are funded by companies that have something to gain from undermining scientific consensus and sowing distrust in science.

- **RULE 9:** Beware of cognitive biases, such as your own negativity, availability, and confirmation biases.

- **RULE 10:** If you read or see something that is very compelling and confirms everything you already believe, make sure the information is coming from a source that is nonpartisan (not affiliated with a political party or identity) and that it doesn't play on a political bias or social identity of yours.

- **RULE 11:** Politicians don't always tell the truth. Sometimes their knowledge of science lets them down, sometimes they follow a misguided party line, and sometimes they have a vested interest in spreading disinformation or obscuring part of the facts.

- **RULE 12:** Beware of medical products and scientific ideas promoted by celebrities.

- **RULE 13:** If you are doubtful about a medical issue, see what the FDA, WHO, and CDC have to say. They represent the most up-to-date and accurate scientific findings, are free from outside interference, and are staffed by first-rate scientists who are charged with protecting our public health.

- **RULE 14:** If a study used human subjects, check to see whether they used a placebo-controlled double-blind clinical trial. The size of the trial is also important because when more patients are enrolled, safety issues and beneficial effects are seen sooner and the differences between the patients with the real medication and those with the placebo are more obvious. Clinical trials can have thousands of subjects, but some scientific studies involving humans are much smaller and should address how they have achieved the statistical confidence they claim to have.

THE TWENTY RULES

- **RULE 15:** Ask yourself what evidence would convince you to change your mind. If there is no evidence, then beware of your own critical thinking.

- **RULE 16:** To sell their medical products and procedures, medical scammers often use testimonials of patients. Beware of medical products that sound unbelievably good and that claim to cure many different diseases. Testimonials are not a substitute for scientific proof, and real doctors would never promise results, because health is impossible to guarantee.

- **RULE 17:** If a supplement tries to look like a medicine, beware.

- **RULE 18:** Beware of clinics that use high-pressure sales techniques to recruit their patients, which include on-the-spot discounts, emotional patient-testimonial videos, and slick recruitment videos.

- **RULE 19:** TV hosts and journalists generate a substantial amount of fake news. To get our attention, morning shows and talk shows need something exciting and new, and not necessarily correct, to report on. Entertainers such as Oz, Dr. Phil (McGraw), and Dr. Drew (Pinsky) should not be your go-to medical sources.

- **RULE 20:** Be wary of promotions using words such as "scientific breakthrough," "miraculous cure," "secret ingredient," and "ancient remedy" and claims that the product is "natural" or "nontoxic" (which doesn't necessarily mean safe). Remember that not all chemicals are bad and that not everything natural is good.

GLOSSARY

attribution science: a new area of science that investigates the links between climate change and extreme weather. It allows scientists to calculate the probability that a certain weather event is due to man-made climate change.

availability bias: a cognitive bias in which people give their own memories and experiences more credence than they deserve. People will overestimate the likelihood of something happening because a similar event has happened recently or has happened to them in particular.

bot: a computer algorithm that performs repetitive tasks, such as resharing and retweeting inflammatory materials

causation: the action of causing an event

charlatan: someone practicing deception to obtain fame, money, or other advantages

citizen science: public participation and collaboration in scientific research

clickbait: fake science (or any other content) with the main purpose of getting internet users to click on a link to a particular web page

climate change: long-term changes in weather due to increased concentrations of greenhouse gases in the atmosphere. Carbon dioxide and methane levels have increased due to fossil fuel combustion and livestock production.

cognitive bias: a series of systematic errors humans make in judgment that can result in overlooking or believing fake science

confirmation bias: a cognitive bias in which people favor, recall, search for, and interpret data in such a way that it favors their preexisting theories, values, and beliefs

correlation: a statistical term used to describe the relationship between two sets of numbers or variables. When one value decreases and the other increases, it is a negative correlation. If both increase together, it is a positive correlation. The stronger the correlation, the closer two variables are linked. Just because two variables are correlated does not mean that the one causes the other.

disinformation: fake information distributed to purposely mislead others. The people who released this information knew it was wrong.

distributed computing framework: a group of computers working together so as to appear as a single computer. Some distributed computing frameworks use the internet to take advantage of volunteers' computers that are sitting idle.

El Niño: a climate pattern that describes unusual warming of the waters of the eastern tropical Pacific. It occurs in an irregular two- to seven-year cycle and can have worldwide climatic consequences.

embryonic stem cells: cells derived from an embryo when it is just a few days old that can differentiate (change) into any cell type and can self-renew (make copies of themselves)

empirical: gained from experimentation and observation

fake news: false stories that appear to be real news

genes: genetic material (DNA) that codes for a protein

genetically modified organism: an organism whose genetic material has been modified in the lab; also called GMO. Genes can be added, removed, or changed.

genetic engineering: the deliberate manipulation of the characteristics of a living thing by altering its DNA

genome: all the genetic material of a cell

gravitational waves: ripples in space-time caused by accelerating massive objects such as neutron stars or black holes orbiting each other. They are invisible, travel at the speed of light, and squeeze and stretch anything in their path.

greenhouse gases: gases that absorb thermal infrared radiation. Increased concentrations of greenhouse gases are responsible for climate change. Carbon dioxide, methane, and water vapor are the main greenhouse gases.

herd immunity: the indirect protection from infectious disease that occurs when a significant fraction of the population has become immune to infection through vaccination or previous infection

lobbyist: a person who tries to influence legislation on behalf of a special interest, such as a pharmaceutical company. Lobbyists get paid to win favor from politicians.

misinformation: fake information distributed inadvertently. The people releasing this information did not know it was wrong.

model organisms: nonhuman organisms that are easily bred and maintained in the lab. Scientists use model organisms, such as mice, with the hope that discoveries made in them will provide insight into the workings of other more complex species, particularly humans.

negativity bias: a cognitive bias in which people are more likely to believe, react to, and remember negative events rather than positive or neutral ones

organic: any molecules containing carbon, even if they have been made in the laboratory; natural, grown without synthetic pesticides, or derived from living matter

parabiosis: a connection between two animals in which they share their blood circulation. In mice it has been shown that blood from a young mouse will rejuvenate an older mouse.

peer-reviewed journals: journals that publish research that has been vetted by other independent experts

placebo effect: the phenomenon that a beneficial health outcome results from an ineffective treatment because the patient believes the treatment is real and will work

predatory journals: journals that look just like peer-reviewed journals but that publish fake science at a cost

preprints: research articles made public by the authors on preprint servers before they have gone through peer review

protein: large biological molecules that do most of the work in cells. They are responsible for the structure, functioning, and regulation of cells.

quackery: the practice of dubious medicine by someone who does not have medical training

stem cells: cells that can differentiate to become specialized cells with a more specific function, such as rod cells in the eye or bone cells

supplements: products taken by mouth that contain a "dietary ingredient"—vitamins, minerals, amino acids, and herbs or botanicals—as well as other substances that can be used to supplement one's diet

synthetic: a material made in the lab or by an industry, not by nature. It could be something that can't be made naturally, such as plastics, or something that does occur naturally, such as sugar.

toxic: something poisonous. All chemicals are toxic. It is just a question of concentration. Even water is toxic if you drink too much of it.

troll: a person who instigates discord on the internet by starting arguments and posting inflammatory statements

university press release: an official statement by a university public relations professional delivered to members of the news media to pique their interest in research done at the university

vaccine: an administered substance that protects people against particular infectious diseases by providing active acquired immunity

wellness: practicing healthy habits daily to improve one's mental and physical health

SOURCE NOTES

10   Isaac Newton, *The Correspondence of Isaac Newton, Volume 1, 1661–1675*, ed. H. W. Turnbull (Cambridge: Cambridge University Press for the Royal Society, 1959), 416.

11   Neil Gershenfeld, "2017: What Scientific Term or Concept Ought to Be More Widely Known?," *Edge*, January 1, 2017, https://www.edge.org/response-detail/27116/; John Brockman, *This Idea Is Brilliant: Lost, Overlooked, and Underappreciated Scientific Concepts Everyone Should Know* (New York: Harper Perennial, 2018), 305.

13   James Somers, "The Scientific Paper Is Obsolete," *Atlantic*, April 5, 2018, https://www.theatlantic.com/science/archive/2018/04/the-scientific-paper-is-obsolete/556676/.

17   Alan Finkel, "Science Isn't Broken, but We Can Do Better: Here's How," Conversation, April 17, 2018, https://theconversation.com/science-isnt-broken-but-we-can-do-better-heres-how-95139/.

21   Laura Spinney, "Germany's COVID-19 Expert: 'For Many, I Am the Evil Guy Crippling the Economy,'" *Guardian* (US edition), April 26, 2020, https://www.theguardian.com/world/2020/apr/26/virologist-christian-drosten-germany-coronavirus-expert-interview/.

23   Laura Stampler, "A Stinky Compound May Protect against Cell Damage, Study Finds," *Time*, July 11, 2014, https://time.com/2976464/rotten-eggs-hydrogen-sulfide-mitochondria/.

29   Soroush Vosoughi, Deb Roy, and Sinan Aral, "The Spread of True and False News Online," *Science* 359, no. 6380 (March 9, 2018): 1146–1151, https://science.sciencemag.org/content/359/6380/1146.full.

31   Tedros Adhanom Ghebreyesus, "Munich Security Conference," opening speech, World Health Organization, February 15, 2020, https://www.who.int/director-general/speeches/detail/munich-security-conference/.

33   "Clickbait," *Oxford Learner's Dictionary*, accessed April 16, 2021, https://www.oxfordlearnersdictionaries.com/definition/english/clickbait/.

34   John Hill, *Cautions against the Immoderate Use of Snuff. Founded on the Known Qualities of the Tobacco Plant: And the Effects It Must Produce When This Way Taken into the Body; And Enforced by Instances of Persons Who Have Perished Miserably of Diseases, Occasioned, Or Rendered Incurable by Its Use* (London: Printed for R. Baldwin in Pater-Noster Row, and J. Jackson in St. James's Street, 1761), https://collections.nlm.nih.gov/bookviewer?PID=nlm:nlmuid-2166041R-bk#page/1/mode/2up/.

34 David Michaels, *Doubt Is Their Product: How Industry's Assault on Science Threatens Your Health* (New York: Oxford University Press, 2008), 11.

36 Michael Shermer, "Consilience and Consensus: Or Why Climate Skeptics Are Wrong," *Scientific American*, December 2015, https://michaelshermer.com/sciam-columns/consilience-and-consensus/.

46 Svante Arrhenius, "On the Influence of Carbonic Acid in the Air upon the Temperature of the Ground," *Philosophical Magazine and Journal of Science* 5, no. 41 (April 1896): 237–276, https://www.rsc.org/images/Arrhenius1896_tcm18-173546.pdf.

48 Robert Brulle, "30 Years Ago Global Warming Became Front-Page News—and Both Republicans and Democrats Took It Seriously," Conversation, June 19, 2018, https://theconversation.com/30-years-ago-global-warming-became-front-page-news-and-both-republicans-and-democrats-took-it-seriously-97658.

52 "Public and Scientists' Views on Science and Society," Pew Research Center, January 29, 2015, https://www.pewresearch.org/science/2015/01/29/public-and-scientists-views-on-science-and-society/.

53 James Painter and Teresa Ashe, "Cross-National Comparison of the Presence of Climate Scepticism in the Print Media in Six Countries, 2007–10," *Environmental Research Letters* 7, no. 4 (October 4, 2012), https://iopscience.iop.org/article/10.1088/1748-9326/7/4/044005/.

54 Hans Rosling, Ola Rosling, and Ana Rosling Rönnlund, *Factfulness: Ten Reasons We're Wrong about the World—and Why Things Are Better Than You Think* (New York: Flatiron Books, 2018), 141.

55 Kate Marvel, "Why I Won't Debate Science," *Hot Planet* (blog), *Scientific American*, June 14, 2018, https://blogs.scientificamerican.com/hot-planet/why-i-wont-debate-science/.

56 Quirin Schiermeier, "Droughts, Heatwaves and Floods: How to Tell When Climate Change Is to Blame," *Nature*, July 30, 2018, https://www.nature.com/articles/d41586-018-05849-9/.

59 Edmund Massey, "A Sermon against the Dangerous and Sinful Practice of Inoculation," Text Creation Partnership, July 8, 1722, https://quod.lib.umich.edu/e/evans/N02782.0001.001?rgn=main;view=fulltext/.

61 Sarah Boseley, "*Lancet* Retracts 'Utterly False' MMR Paper," *Guardian* (US edition), February 2, 2010, https://www.theguardian.com/society/2010/feb/02/lancet-retracts-mmr-paper/.

62 Sarah Boseley, "How Disgraced Anti-Vaxxer Andrew Wakefield Was Embraced by Trump's America," *Guardian* (US edition), July 18, 2018, https://www.theguardian.com/society/2018/jul/18/how-disgraced-anti-vaxxer-andrew-wakefield-was-embraced-by-trumps-america/.

63   Rosling, *Factfulness*, 116.

65   Jennifer Reich, "What's Wrong with Those Anti-Vaxxers? They're Just Like the Rest of Us," Conversation, May 22, 2019, https://theconversation.com/whats-wrong-with-those-anti-vaxxers-theyre-just-like-the-rest-of-us-117548/.

66   Matthew Motta, Dominik Stecuła, and Kathryn Haglin, "Countering Misinformation about Flu Vaccine Is Harder Than It Seems," Conversation, December 6, 2018, https://theconversation.com/countering-misinformation-about-flu-vaccine-is-harder-than-it-seems-106479/.

68   Michael Gerson, "Are You Anti-GMO? Then You're Anti-Science, Too," *Washington Post*, May 3, 2018, https://www.washingtonpost.com/opinions/are-you-anti-gmo-then-youre-anti-science-too/2018/05/03/cb42c3ba-4ef4-11e8-af46-b1d6dc0d9bfe_story.html.

71   Seth Borenstein, "GMOs Not Harmful to Human Health, Major Study Concludes," KQED, May 17, 2016, https://www.kqed.org/stateofhealth/185632/gmos-not-harmful-to-human-health/.

74   Claire Benjamin, "Scientists Engineer Shortcut for Photosynthetic Glitch, Boost Crop Growth 40%," Carl R. Woese Institute for Genomic Biology, January 3, 2019, https://www.igb.illinois.edu/article/scientists-engineer-shortcut-photosynthetic-glitch-boost-crop-growth-40.

75   Rosling, *Factfulness*, 117.

75   Michael Gerson, "Michael Gerson: A Contempt for Science Can Have a Human Cost," *Spokane Spokesman Review*, May 4, 2018, https://www.spokesman.com/stories/2018/may/04/michael-gerson-a-contempt-for-science-can-have-a-h/.

78   Robert Talbor and Nicolas de Blégny, "The English Remedy, or, Talbor's Wonderful Secret for the Cureing of Agues and Feavers—Sold by the Author, Sir Robert Talbor to the Most Christian King and since His Death Ordered by His Majesty to Be Published in French, for the Benefit of His Subjects; and Now Translated into English for Publick Good" (London: Printed by J. Wallis for Jos. Hindmarsh, 1682), available online at Oxford Text Archive, https://ota.bodleian.ox.ac.uk/repository/xmlui/handle/20.500.12024/A62495/.

79   Jessica Leigh Hester, "When Quackery on the Radio Was a Public Health Crisis," Atlas Obscura, January 12, 2018, https://www.atlasobscura.com/articles/quackery-radio-public-health-crisis-medicine-regulators-miracle-cures/.

80–81 "Prevagen Improves Memory," Prevagen, accessed April 16, 2021, https://www.prevagen.com/about-prevagen/.

81   "Prevagen."

81   Barbara Gabriel, "AARP Asks Court to Declare Prevagen Ads Misleading," AARP, March 21, 2018, https://www.aarp.org/politics-society/advocacy/info-2018/overturn-prevagen-decision-fd.html.

85 "FDA Warns about Stem Cell Therapies," FDA, September 3, 2019, https://www.fda.gov/ForConsumers/ConsumerUpdates/ucm286155.htm.

86 University of California, Santa Barbara, "Cells Treat Macular Degeneration," ScienceDaily, March 19, 2018, https://www.sciencedaily.com/releases/2018/03/180319124218.htm.

88 Laurie McGinley and William Wan, "Miracle Cures or Modern Quackery? Stem Cell Clinics Multiply, with Heartbreaking Results for Some Patients," *Washington Post*, April 29, 2018, https://www.washingtonpost.com/national/health-science/miracle-cures-or-modern-quackery-stem-cell-clinics-multiply-with-heartbreaking-results-for-some-patients/2018/04/29/80cbcee8-26e1-11e8-874b-d517e912f125_story.html.

88 McGinley and Wan.

89 Clive M. McCay, F. Pope, and Wanda Lunsford, "Experimental Prolongation of the Life Span," *Bulletin of the New York Academy of Medicine* 32, no. 2 (February 1, 1956), 91–101.

89–90 Megan Scudellari, "Blood to Blood," *Nature* 517 (January 22, 2015): 426–429, https://www.nature.com/news/polopoly_fs/1.16762!/menu/main/topColumns/topLeftColumn/pdf/517426a.pdf.

90 Scudellari.

90 Jocelyn Kaiser, "Young Blood Antiaging Trial Raises Questions," *Science*, August 1, 2016, https://www.sciencemag.org/news/2016/08/young-blood-antiaging-trial-raises-questions/.

90 Michael Easter, "People Are Getting Transfusions with Young People's Blood to Fight Aging," *Men's Health*, January 18, 2019, https://www.menshealth.com/health/a25949234/young-blood-transfusions-anti-aging/.

92 Rebecca Robbins, "How a Society Gala Was Used to Sell Young-Blood Transfusions to Baby Boomers Desperate to Cheat Death," Stat, March 2, 2018, https://www.statnews.com/2018/03/02/young-blood-anti-aging-study/.

92 Linda Keslar, "The Rise of Fake Medical News," Proto, June 18, 2018, http://protomag.com/articles/rise-fake-medical-news/.

93 Maki Inoue-Choi, Sarah Oppeneer, and Kim Robien, "Reality Check: There Is No Such Thing as a Miracle Food," *Nutrition and Cancer* 65, no. 2 (2013), 165–168, https://www.ncbi.nlm.nih.gov/pmc/articles/PMC3635479/.

93 Bill Briggs, "Dr. Oz Responds to Critics: 'It's Not a Medical Show,'" NBC News, April 23, 2015, https://www.nbcnews.com/health/health-news/dr-oz-responds-critics-its-not-medical-show-n347101/.

94 "Your Personal Health Horoscope," *The Dr. Oz Show*, season 9, episode 167, CBS, June 6, 2018.

95–96 Heidi Ledford, "Chloroquine Hype Is Derailing the Search for Coronavirus Treatments," *Nature* 580, no. 7805 (April 2020), https://www.nature.com/articles/d41586-020-01165-3/.

96–97 Erin Biba, "Why Are So Many Women Rejecting Medical Science?," Dame, April 22, 2019, https://www.damemagazine .com/2019/2004/2022/why-are-so-many-women-rejecting -medical-science/.

97 Biba.

97 Caroline Rothstein, "The Wellness Industry Isn't Making You Well," *Marie Claire*, January 1, 2019, https://www.marieclaire .com/health-fitness/a23652473/wellness-industry-problems/.

97–98 Jen Gunter, "Worshiping the False Idols of Wellness," *New York Times*, August 1, 2018, https://www.nytimes.com/2018/08/01 /style/wellness-industrial-complex.html.

98 Amanda Suazo, "9 Activated Charcoal Recipes to Detox from the Inside Out," Bulletproof, accessed January 28, 2019, https://blog .bulletproof.com/activated-charcoal-recipes-2b3c4t5c/.

SELECTED BIBLIOGRAPHY

Brulle, Robert. "30 Years Ago Global Warming Became Front-Page News—and Both Republicans and Democrats Took It Seriously." Conversation, June 19, 2018. https://theconversation.com/30-years-ago -global-warming-became-front-page-news-and-both-republicans-and -democrats-took-it-seriously-97658.

Funk, Cary, and Brian Kennedy. "Public Knowledge about Science Has a Limited Tie to People's Beliefs about Climate Change and Climate Scientists." Pew Research Center, October 4, 2016. https://www .pewresearch.org/science/2016/10/04/public-knowledge-about-science -has-a-limited-tie-to-peoples-beliefs-about-climate-change-and-climate -scientists/.

Gunter, Jen. "Worshiping the False Idols of Wellness." *New York Times*, August 1, 2018. https://www.nytimes.com/2018/08/01/style/wellness -industrial-complex.html.

"Health & Fitness." Federal Trade Commission. Accessed April 16, 2021. https://www.consumer.ftc.gov/health.

"Health Fraud Scams." US Food & Drug Administration, March 11, 2021. https://www.fda.gov/ForConsumers/ProtectYourself/HealthFraud/default .htm.

Hester, Jessica Leigh. "When Quackery on the Radio Was a Public Health Crisis." Atlas Obscura, January 12, 2018. https://www.atlasobscura.com /articles/quackery-radio-public-health-crisis-medicine-regulators-miracle -cures/.

Kang, Lydia, and Nate Pedersen. *Quackery: A Brief History of the Worst Ways to Cure Everything.* New York: Workman, 2017.

Keslar, Linda. "The Rise of Fake Medical News." Proto, June 18, 2018. http://protomag.com/articles/rise-fake-medical-news/.

Korownyk, Christina, Michael R. Kolber, James McCormack, Vanessa Lam, Kate Overbo, Candra Cotton, Caitlin Finley, et al. "Televised Medical Talk Shows—What They Recommend and the Evidence to Support Their Recommendations: A Prospective Observational Study." *British Medical Journal* 349, no. g7346 (December 17, 2014). https://www.bmj.com /content/349/bmj.g7346/.

Marshall, George. *Don't Even Think about It: Why Our Brains Are Wired to Ignore Climate Change.* New York: Bloomsbury USA, 2015.

Mnookin, Seth. *The Panic Virus: The True Story behind the Vaccine-Autism Controversy.* New York: Simon and Schuster, 2012.

Otto, Shawn. *The War on Science: Who's Waging It, Why It Matters, What We Can Do about It.* Minneapolis: Milkweed Editions, 2016.

Rothstein, Caroline. "The Wellness Industry Isn't Making You Well." *Marie Claire*, January 1, 2019. https://www.marieclaire.com/health-fitness/a23652473/wellness-industry-problems/.

Sumner, Petroc, Solveiga Vivian-Griffiths, Jacky Boivin, Andy Williams, Christos A. Venetis, Aimée Davies, Jack Ogden, et al. "The Association between Exaggeration in Health Related Science News and Academic Press Releases: Retrospective Observational Study." *British Medical Journal* 349, no. g7015 (December 10, 2014). https://www.bmj.com/content/349/bmj.g7015/.

Vosoughi, Soroush, Deb Roy, and Sinan Aral. "The Spread of True and False News Online." *Science* 359, no. 6380 (March 9, 2018): 1146–1151. https://science.sciencemag.org/content/359/6380/1146.full.

Zimmer, Marc. *The State of Science: What the Future Holds and the Scientists Making It Happen*. Guilford, CT: Prometheus, 2020.

FURTHER INFORMATION

Books

Haelle, Tara. *Vaccination Investigation: The History and Science of Vaccines*. Minneapolis: Twenty-First Century Books, 2018.

McPherson, Stephanie Sammartino. *Hothouse Earth: The Climate Crisis and the Importance of Carbon Neutrality*. Minneapolis: Twenty-First Century Books, 2021.

Miller, Michael. *Fake News: Separating Truth from Fiction*. Minneapolis: Twenty-First Century Books, 2019.

Rosling, Hans, Ola Rosling, and Ana Rosling Rönnlund. *Factfulness: Ten Reasons We're Wrong about the World—and Why Things Are Better Than You Think*. New York: Flatiron Books, 2018.

Zimmer, Marc. *Solutions for a Cleaner, Greener Planet: Environmental Chemistry*. Minneapolis: Twenty-First Century Books, 2019.

Fact-Checking Websites

Beall's List of Potential Predatory Journals and Publishers
https://beallslist.net
Check out this list to make sure any scientific findings you see in the news come from a legitimate source.

FactCheck.org
https://www.factcheck.org
This project of the Annenberg Public Policy Center of the University of Pennsylvania is a nonpartisan, nonprofit consumer advocate for voters that aims to reduce the level of deception and confusion in US politics. It monitors the factual accuracy of what is said by major US political players in TV ads, debates, speeches, interviews, and news releases.

PolitiFact
> https://www.politifact.com
> This fact-checking website rates the accuracy of claims by elected officials and others on its Truth-O-Meter. The project is operated by the Poynter Institute, a nonprofit journalism school and research organization.

Snopes
> https://www.snopes.com
> Formerly known as the Urban Legends Reference Pages, Snopes has been described as the definitive internet reference source for researching urban legends, folklore, myths, rumors, and misinformation.

Truth or Fiction
> https://www.truthorfiction.com
> This website does not primarily provide fact-checking about current events but, instead, addresses wild and amazing claims, pictures, or stories. This is the site to visit if you need to check the veracity of urban legends, internet rumors, and email hoaxes.

Science News Websites

The Conversation: Science and Technology
> https://theconversation.com/us/technology/
> The Conversation is an independent, nonprofit publisher of commentary and analysis, authored by academics and edited by journalists for the general public. They publish short articles by academics on timely topics related to the academics' research.

Nature News
> https://www.nature.com/news/
> Based in the UK and attracting about five hundred thousand readers, *Nature* is one of the world's leading research journals. *Nature* News summarizes some of the most important recent scientific discoveries published in recent journals.

Science: Latest News
> https://www.sciencemag.org/news/latest-news/
> *Science* is one of the world's top peer-reviewed journals. It is published weekly, based in the US, and boasts some five hundred thousand readers. Much like *Nature* News, this site publishes articles about important recent scientific discoveries.

INDEX

ABOUT THE AUTHOR

Marc Zimmer is the author of *The State of Science: What the Future Holds and the Scientists Making It Happen* and several nonfiction young adult books as well as a professor at Connecticut College, where he teaches chemistry and studies the proteins involved in producing light in jellyfish and fireflies. He received his PhD in chemistry from Worcester Polytechnic Institute and did his postdoc at Yale University. He has published articles on science and medicine for the *Los Angeles Times*, *USA Today*, and the Huffington Post, among many other publications. He lives in Waterford, Connecticut, with his wife.

PHOTO ACKNOWLEDGMENTS